The Ami Pro Window's H

MW00768921

Display the Modify Page Layout dialog box

Display the Modify Style dialog box

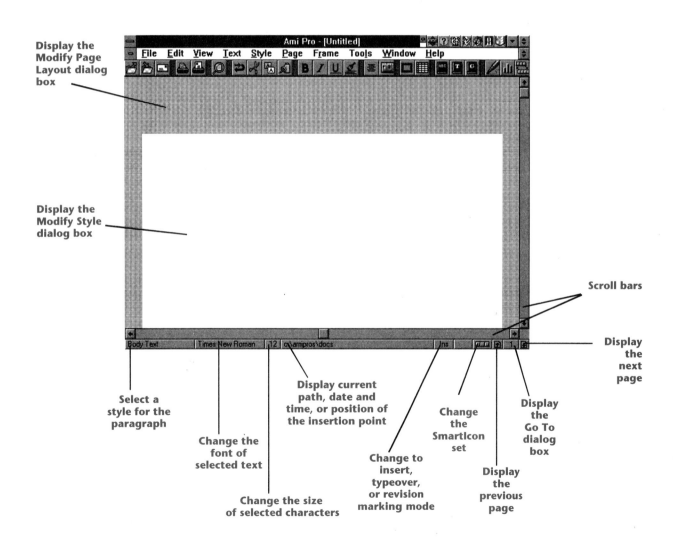

Scroll bars

Display the next page

Select a style for the paragraph

Display current path, date and time, or position of the insertion point

Change the font of selected text

Change the SmartIcon set

Display the Go To dialog box

Change to insert, typeover, or revision marking mode

Display the previous page

Change the size of selected characters

For every kind of computer user, there is a SYBEX book.

All computer users learn in their own way. Some need straightforward and methodical explanations. Others are just too busy for this approach. But no matter what camp you fall into, SYBEX has a book that can help you get the most out of your computer and computer software while learning at your own pace.

Beginners generally want to start at the beginning. The **ABC's** series, with its step-by-step lessons in plain language, helps you build basic skills quickly. Or you might try our **Quick & Easy** series, the friendly, full-color guide.

The **Mastering** and **Understanding** series will tell you everything you need to know about a subject. They're perfect for intermediate and advanced computer users, yet they don't make the mistake of leaving beginners behind.

If you're a busy person and are already comfortable with computers, you can choose from two SYBEX series—**Up & Running** and **Running Start**. The **Up & Running** series gets you started in just 20 lessons. Or you can get two books in one, a step-by-step tutorial and an alphabetical reference, with our **Running Start** series.

Everyone who uses computer software can also use a computer software reference. SYBEX offers the gamut—from portable **Instant References** to comprehensive **Encyclopedias**, **Desktop References**, and **Bibles**.

SYBEX even offers special titles on subjects that don't neatly fit a category—like **Tips & Tricks**, the **Shareware Treasure Chests**, and a wide range of books for Macintosh computers and software.

SYBEX books are written by authors who are expert in their subjects. In fact, many make their living as professionals, consultants or teachers in the field of computer software. And their manuscripts are thoroughly reviewed by our technical and editorial staff for accuracy and ease-of-use.

So when you want answers about computers or any popular software package, just help yourself to SYBEX.

For a complete catalog of our publications, please write:

SYBEX Inc.
2021 Challenger Drive
Alameda, CA 94501
Tel: (510) 523-8233/(800) 227-2346 Telex: 336311
Fax: (510) 523-2373

TALK TO SYBEX ONLINE.

THE PUSHBUTTON GUIDE™ TO

LOTUS® SMARTSUITE®

Sheila S. Dienes

SYBEX®

San Francisco · Paris · Düsseldorf · Soest

PUSHBUTTON GUIDE BOOK CONCEPT: David Kolodney
DEVELOPMENTAL EDITOR: Sarah Wadsworth
EDITOR: Abby Azrael
TECHNICAL EDITOR: Adebisi Oladipupo
BOOK DESIGNER: Claudia Smelser
PRODUCTION ARTIST: Lisa Jaffe
TYPESETTER: Thomas Goudie
PROOFREADER/PRODUCTION ASSISTANT: Kate Westrich
INDEXER: Nancy Guenther
COVER DESIGNER: Archer Design

Some screen reproductions produced with Collage Plus.

Collage Plus is a trademark of Inner Media Inc.

SYBEX is a registered trademark of SYBEX Inc.

TRADEMARKS: SYBEX has attempted throughout this book to distinguish proprietary trademarks from descriptive terms by following the capitalization style used by the manufacturer.

Every effort has been made to supply complete and accurate information. However, SYBEX assumes no responsibility for its use, nor for any infringement of the intellectual property rights of third parties which would result from such use.

Library of Congress Card Number: 94-67533
ISBN: 0-7821-1603-5

Manufactured in the United States of America
10 9 8 7 6 5 4 3 2 1

To Mary and Art Dienes

cknowledgments

I would like to take this opportunity to extend my sincere thanks to all who helped produce this book. Thanks to Dr. Rudolph Langer, Barbara Gordon, Joanne Cuthbertson, and everyone at SYBEX who made this book possible.

My thanks to developmental editor Sarah Wadsworth for offering me the opportunity to write this book and for her wise advice concerning its content. My special thanks to editor Abby Azrael for her close attention to the many details in this book, for her infinite patience, and for her sensible observations. I also want to thank Michelle Khazai for working on the poster inside the back cover of the book.

In addition, I wish to extend a hearty "Thank you" to the following people: technical reviewer Adebisi Oladipupo; book designer Claudia Smelser; production artist Lisa Jaffe; typesetter Thomas Goudie; proofreader Kate Westrich; and indexer Nancy Guenther.

 oolbar Buttons at a Glance

SmartCenter SmartIcons

Start Lotus 1-2-3 **22, 38**

Start Lotus Ami Pro **132, 144, 334**

Start Lotus Approach **212, 228**

Start Lotus Freelance Graphics **270**

Start Lotus Organizer **318, 338**

Lotus 1-2-3 SmartIcons

Align Left **53**

Align Right **53, 60**

Bold **56, 60**

Center **53**

Center All **118**

Lotus 1-2-3 SmartIcons

Center Horizontally **117**

Column Print Titles **116**

Center Vertically **118**

Column Width **61**

Chart **98**

Copy **41, 72**

Chart Type **102**

Cut **41, 72**

Close **126**

Delete **44, 45, 86**

Lotus 1-2-3 SmartIcons

Delete Columns **65, 77**

Facing Pages **125**

Delete Rows **65**

Fast Format **59**

Delete Styles **59**

Horizontal Page Break **115**

Drop Shadow **63**

Insert Columns **65**

Enlarge **124**

Insert Rows **64**

Lotus 1-2-3 SmartIcons

Italic **56**

Landscape Orientation **117**

Lines, Borders, and Colors **63**

Multiple Pages **126**

Next Page **124**

Next Set **61**

Open **38, 98**

Page Layout **119, 121, 123, 125**

Paste **41, 72**

Pie Chart **104**

Lotus 1-2-3
SmartIcons

Portrait Orientation **117**

Row Print Titles **117**

Previous Page **124**

Save **30, 33, 45**

Print **126**

Sequence **29**

Print Preview **124**

Single Page **125**

Reduce **125**

Size Columns **118**

Lotus 1-2-3
SmartIcons

Size Data **118**

Size Rows **118**

Sum **79**

3D Pie Chart **104**

3D Vertical Bar Chart **104**

Vertical Area Chart **104**

Vertical Bar Chart **104**

Vertical Line Chart **104**

Vertical Page Break **115**

Underline **56**

Lotus 1-2-3 SmartIcons

 LT05C055.TIF

Undo **45**

Ami Pro SmartIcons

 AM03C362.TIF

Add Frame **187, 189**

 AM03C073.TIF

Bold **160, 190**

 AM03C402.TIF

Bring to Front **193**

 AM03C074.TIF

Center **161, 180**

 LT05C057.TIF

Copy **151, 192**

 LT05C056.TIF

Cut **151, 191**

 LT05C065.TIF

Fast Format **168, 169**

 AM03C156.TIF

Group **194**

Ami Pro SmartIcons

Import Picture **188**

Italic **160, 190**

Justify **161**

Modify Frame Layout **195, 196**

Modify Page Layout **179, 183**

Open **144, 159**

Page Break **181**

Page Number **182**

Paste **151, 152, 191, 192**

Print **201, 205, 206**

Ami Pro SmartIcons

Print Envelope **203**

Save **138, 139, 150, 172**

Send to Back **193**

Show Ruler **162**

Toggle Full Page/Layout View **200, 206**

Underline **160**

Undo **154**

Ungroup **194**

Approach SmartIcons

Add Field **236**

Approach SmartIcons

Align Left **264**

Align Right **264**

All Records **246, 248**

Browse **220, 244, 254**

Center **255, 264**

Change Style & Properties
238, 256, 262

Comma **247**

Date **221**

Design **262**

Drawing Tools **236, 263**

Approach
SmartIcons

Duplicate Record **221**

Enter **221, 232, 235**

Equal To **245**

Fast Format **240**

Find Set **245, 246**

First Record **233, 235**

Last Record **233**

Less Than **246**

Next Record **233**

New Record **220**

Approach
SmartIcons

Not Equal To **246**

Save **222, 223, 254**

Open **228**

Select **264**

Preview **262**

Show Gridlines **240**

Previous Record **233**

Show Rulers **240**

Print **260, 265**

Sort Ascending **248, 257**

Approach SmartIcons

Sort Descending **248**

Text Block **263**

Underline **241, 263**

Freelance Graphics SmartIcons

Add Symbol **292**

Bold **290**

Collapse Outline **304**

Collapse Page **304**

Color **308**

Copy **302**

Approach SmartIcons

Approach
SmartIcons

Approach SmartIcons

Zoom Page **289**

Organizer SmartIcons

Exit

New **329**

New Entry **325**

Open **339**

Save **329**

Working Together Bonus Pack

Collect & Copy for 1-2-3 **335**

Collect & Copy for Freelance **337**

Working Together Bonus Pack

Contents at a Glance

Table of Contents

CHAPTER 4 **Formatting Your
Worksheet and Data** **51**

PART THREE *Ami Pro* 129

CHAPTER 9 **Creating a Document** 131

CHAPTER 10 **Editing a Document** 143

CHAPTER 11 Formatting Document Text   157

ntroduction

Lotus SmartSuite is a group of the most useful Windows applications you can buy. With Lotus SmartSuite, you can perform virtually every task you can think of on your computer. The SmartSuite applications are Lotus 1-2-3, an electronic spreadsheet; Ami Pro, a word-processing program with graphic capabilities; Lotus Approach, a database program; Freelance Graphics, used to create presentations; and Lotus Organizer, a personal information manager.

The applications in Lotus SmartSuite can be integrated. For example, you can easily copy the data entered in one application to another SmartSuite application to create a document, worksheet, or presentation. In fact, that is one of the best reasons to use SmartSuite—the applications work so well together!

Why Use This Book?

This book will quickly get you started working in each of the SmartSuite applications. Read Chapter 1 to become familiar with the SmartSuite interface. Then, you can read each of the sections to see the similarities among each of the applications. Finally, you can use the book to refresh your memory as to how to quickly accomplish a specific task when you create your own projects using the SmartSuite.

In this book, the SmartIcons, status bar buttons, and quick menus appear in the margins beside the steps necessary to carry out a task. In fact, you can practically follow the steps by just looking at the graphics in the margins—in many cases you won't even need to read the steps.

The SmartIcons are such an important part of the SmartSuite that a wonderful poster containing many of the SmartIcons is included in the back of this book. Use the poster for reference when you need to find out how to carry out an action in one of the SmartSuite applications.

In addition, you can check the special SmartIcons Table of Contents to quickly locate the page number(s) upon which a specific SmartIcon button is discussed. Some of the buttons change appearance slightly depending on whether their feature is "turned on."

Conventions Used in This Book

Because this book is about using hot spots and buttons to perform your tasks, you don't often need to pull down the main menus in any of the applications. However, there are a few times when it may be convenient to use commands on the main menus.

Commands that are selected from one of the pull-down menus on the menu bar will be abbreviated as *Menu Name* ➤ *Command Name*. For example, if a step tells you to select Tools ➤ SmartIcons, then click on the Tools menu on the menu bar and click on the SmartIcons command on the pull-down menu. If the abbreviated command also contains a key sequence in parentheses, such as File ➤ Open (Ctrl+O), then you can either select the command on the pull-down menu or use the key sequence to access the command. In this case, you could press and hold down the Ctrl key, and then press O to access the command.

> **TIP**
>
> **Be sure you check out the Notes, Tips, and Warnings that appear throughout the book. They contain important information about the preceding step or action.**

Some Terms You'll Need to Know

This book is designed to show you the easiest way to accomplish a wide variety of tasks in each SmartSuite application. Some (but not much) terminology is necessary to guide you through the process.

The following is a brief definition of terms used in this book:

Click   Press and quickly release the left (primary) mouse button.

Double-click   Click the left mouse button twice in rapid succession.

Right-click   Press and quickly release the right (non-primary) mouse button.

Drag   Press and hold down the left mouse button. Then move the mouse to a different location and release the button.

Select   Click on data or objects (such as a menu command), or drag through data to *highlight* it when you want to perform some action on it.

Highlight   Select data so it appears on your screen in reverse video. For example, selected text appears with white characters on a black background.

Selected check box   Click on a *cleared* (empty) check box to choose the option indicated beside the check box. A selected check box appears with an "X" or a check mark in it.

Cleared check box   Click on a selected check box to remove the "X" or a check mark. A cleared check box's option is not in effect.

Installing Lotus SmartSuite

When you are ready to install Lotus SmartSuite, allow a two-hour block of time for the installation process. The SmartSuite package comes with more than 20 disks to use during the installation, but the process is almost totally automatic. Once you are finished with the installation, each of the SmartSuite applications is ready to run.

To install and be able to run all the SmartSuite programs, you must have a 386 computer with at least 4MB of memory and Windows 3.1. If you want to run more than one application at a time, you might want to have additional memory in your computer.

To completely install Lotus SmatSuite, you'll need up to 86MB of hard disk space for your data files.

Follow these steps to install Lotus SmartSuite:

1. If necessary, type **WIN** at the C:\> prompt to start Windows.

2. Insert Disk 1 into your A: or B: drive.

3. Select Program Manager's File ➤ Run command.

4. Type **a:install** or **b:install** in the Command Line text box.

5. Click on OK to begin the installation

6. When prompted, type your name and your company name in the text boxes and then click on Next. You must type something in the Company Name text box to proceed with the installation. Click on Yes in the Confirm Names dialog box.

7. Install suggests a drive and directory name in which to install each SmartSuite application. Click on Next to accept the suggestions.

8. When Install suggests that each application's icon be placed in the Lotus Applications group, click on OK.

9. Click on Yes when Install asks if you want to begin copying the SmartSuite files. As requested by Install, enter each disk in succesion and click on OK.

10. Click on Yes to have Install update your AUOTEXEC.BAT file. Then remove the last installation disk from your floppy drive and click on Restart to boot your computer with the new AUTOEXEC.BAT file.

That's it, and it was not too difficult. Now you can get started working in Lotus SmartSuite.

1

Introduction to Lotus SmartSuite

CHAPTER ONE

Introducing
Lotus SmartSuite

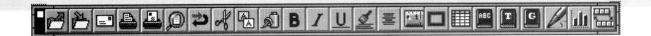

LOTUS SMARTSUITE IS a set of Windows applications you can use to produce professional-looking spreadsheets, text documents, graphics presentations, and databases. But SmartSuite goes even further than the individual applications within it. It includes the Lotus SmartCenter application, which allows you to start one of the SmartSuite applications at any time by clicking on its button on the SmartCenter button bar, and the "Working Together" package, which allows you to easily combine data already entered in one application with data in any of its other applications.

One major advantage to using Lotus SmartSuite is that each of its applications contains the same *user interface*, a set of commands used to produce results in a program. Once you learn one program, you'll be familiar with each of the others—a great time-saver!

The SmartSuite Components

Lotus SmartSuite includes five of the most useful Windows business applications, as well as the Lotus SmartCenter application and the "Working Together" package so you can easily integrate your data within the SmartSuite applications.

1-2-3 for Windows

Use 1-2-3 for Windows to analyze data, perform calculations, and easily create professional-looking spreadsheets, called *worksheets* in 1-2-3. For example, you can create worksheets for an expense report, a departmental or personal budget, or an investment analysis. 1-2-3's built-in charting capabilities make it easy for you to present worksheet data in a graph.

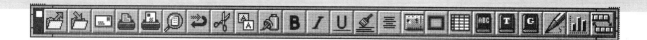

One of 1-2-3's best features is its ability to store related data in a multiple-worksheet file. Keeping related data on different worksheets in the same file can save you time and simplify your work.

Ami Pro

Create all your text documents, such as reports, letters, and even fax cover sheets, with Ami Pro, one of the most user-friendly word processing programs available. With Ami Pro, you can effortlessly create documents that have consistent formatting by assigning a specific style to each paragraph. Ami Pro's graphic features make it simple to enhance your documents with pictures or place text in a frame so it can be moved virtually anywhere on a page.

Approach for Windows

To easily manage a database even if you have no database experience, use Approach for Windows. You can create a list of employee records, a mailing list, or maintain a list of business contacts with Approach. Its relational capabilities enable you to use and combine data in any file format it supports (all the major database formats), and you can analyze, edit, and report on your data.

Freelance Graphics for Windows

Use Freelance Graphics for Windows to produce top-quality graphics presentations on slides, overheads, and handouts. Choose from Freelance Graphics' backgrounds and formats, and then enter the text to create a sales presentation or the visual aids for a class. With Freelance Graphics you can produce uniform results for a professional effect.

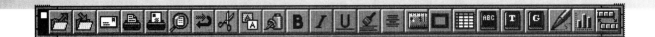

Lotus Organizer

Organizer is a personal information manager (PIM) similar to a date-book. It includes sections containing a calendar, an address list, a notepad, a list of tasks to perform, a yearly planner, and a list of anniversaries. However, Organizer is much more powerful than a datebook—it reminds you of appointments, and automatically places your own To Do list and Anniversaries in your Calendar.

Lotus SmartCenter

Lotus SmartCenter is an application that runs by default each time you start Windows, and appears as a SmartIcon set at the top-right side of your screen. Use buttons on the SmartCenter SmartIcon set to get help about Lotus Smart-Suite, start 1-2-3, Ami Pro, Freelance Graphics, and Approach, display the SmartCenter menu, and customize the SmartCenter SmartIcon set.

Working Together

The Working Together package lets you combine data within the SmartSuite applications. For example, use data in an Ami Pro document to create a presentation with Freelance Graphics, or run the Quick @Function Calculator to use a 1-2-3 @function in an Ami Pro document. The Working Together package is what makes SmartSuite so smart.

Using Windows

Of course, you must have Windows 3.1 (or later) installed on your computer in order to run Lotus SmartSuite 3.0 for Windows. In this book, it is assumed that you are somewhat familiar with using Windows.

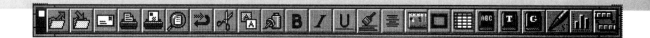

Follow these steps to begin a SmartSuite session:

1. At the C:\> prompt, type **WIN** and press ↵ to start Windows.

2. By default, the Welcome To Lotus SmartSuite dialog box, shown in Figure 1.1, appears the first time you start Windows after installing Lotus SmartSuite.

3. To automatically load the Lotus SmartCenter application each time you start Windows, select the Don't Show This Screen Again check box, and then click on OK.

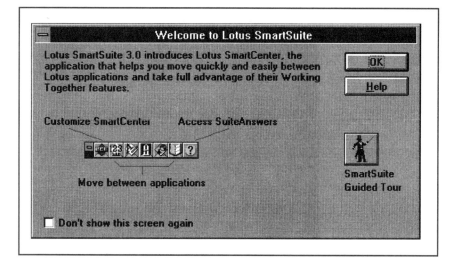

FIGURE 1.1

The Welcome To Lotus SmartSuite dialog box appears the first time you start Windows after Lotus SmartSuite is installed.

The SmartSuite Interface

Each of the applications in Lotus SmartSuite contains similar features in its user interface. For example, all of the applications contain *SmartIcons*,

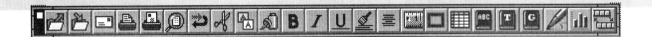

buttons that you "push" (click on) to perform the corresponding command or action. 1-2-3, Ami Pro, Approach, and Freelance Graphics each have an *interactive status bar*, which means you can use buttons on the status bar to perform some additional commands and actions. *Quick menus*, available for 1-2-3, Approach, and Freelance Graphics, let you choose a command that is related to data you have selected.

T I P

Use the SmartIcons, status bar buttons, and quick menus as shortcuts to commands. You can carry out almost every command in each application without ever pulling down the main menus on the menu bar.

Figure 1.2 shows an Ami Pro document window that contains many of the elements of the SmartSuite interface.

The following list describes most of the elements labeled in Figure 1.2:

- The *title bar* indicates the name of the current (active) worksheet, document, database, presentation, or Organizer file.

- The *menu bar* contains the names of the menus from which you can select commands.

- The *SmartIcons* are displayed below the menu bar, but above the area in which data is entered.

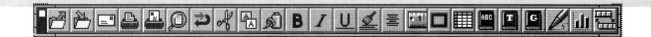

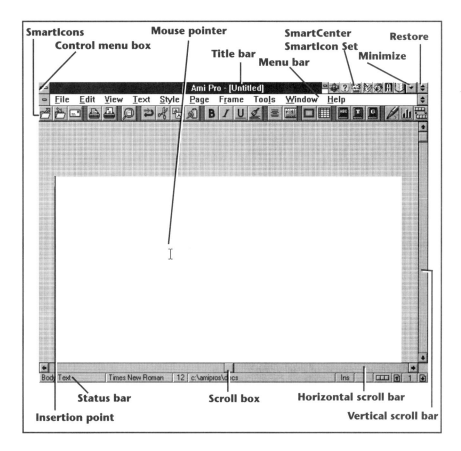

FIGURE 1.2

Many of the elements of the SmartSuite interface appear in the Ami Pro window.

- Both a *horizontal* and a *vertical scroll bar*, each containing a *scroll box*, appear in the window to help you scroll through a long document. Click on the arrow buttons on each scroll bar to display the next or previous screenful of data. Drag the scroll box on the appropriate scroll bar to display a general area of the document.

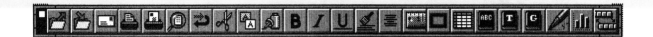

- The *status bar* displays information about the active file. It also contains buttons that allow you to change the format of the selection, hide the SmartIcons or select a different SmartIcon set, and perform specific tasks in each application.

- The *Control menu box* appears on the left side of the title bar. Double-click on it to close the application.

- The *Minimize* and *Restore* buttons appear on the right side of the title bar. Click on the Minimize button to reduce the application to an icon. Click on the Restore button to return the application window to its previous size.

- The *insertion point* appears as a flashing vertical bar. It indicates where the next character you type will appear.

- The *mouse pointer* appears as an arrow when it is pointing to an object. However, it changes shape according to its current function. For example, it appears as an I-beam in an Ami Pro document.

Using the SmartIcons

The SmartIcons appear in a row below the menu bar in each of the SmartSuite applications. 1-2-3, Approach, and Ami Pro come with several *SmartIcon sets*, groups of SmartIcons with related commands. For example, 1-2-3 contains sets of SmartIcons to use while editing, formatting, or printing a worksheet.

You must have a mouse to use the SmartIcons. To use a specific Smart-Icon, it must be displayed on your screen.

T I P

To use a SmartIcon in a set that is not displayed on your
screen, display the set that contains the SmartIcon. First, click
on the SmartIcon button on the status bar to display a list of
available SmartIcon sets, and then click on the name of the set
you want to display.

To use any of the displayed SmartIcons:

- Point to a button to display "bubble help," a reminder of the button's command or function.

- Point to the icon that represents the command or function you want
  to use, and then click on it to carry out the command or action.

N O T E

In Organizer, the description of an icon's function appears in a
bubble beside the icon when you click and hold down the right
mouse button. In 1-2-3 and Approach, just point to the SmartIcon
to display a description of its function in a bubble.

Customizing the SmartIcons

Although each application (except Organizer) comes with at least one defined set of SmartIcons, you can add icons to an existing defined set, create
your own sets, or change the positions of icons on a displayed SmartIcon set.

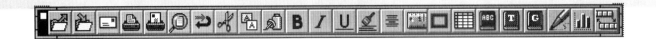

Creating or Customizing a SmartIcon Set

Because the SmartIcons are so easy to use, you may want to customize the set(s) you often display. If you don't want to change the set(s) that came with the application, just create a new set by assigning a new name to a customized set.

1. Start the application that contains the SmartIcon set you want to change. For example, start Ami Pro.

2. Select Tools ➤ SmartIcons from the pull-down menu that appears to display a SmartIcons dialog box similar to that in Figure 1.3.

3. Click on the drop-down button to reveal a list of defined SmartIcon sets, and then select the name of the set you want to customize.

N O T E

Organizer comes with some SmartIcons displayed, but does not contain a defined SmartIcon set. You can add to or remove icons from those displayed. Select Tools ➤ SmartIcons, and then click on Customize. Drag any of the Standard Icons you want to display to the Current Palette area, and then click on OK in the Customize dialog box and again in the Tools SmartIcons dialog box.

4. To add an icon to an existing set, drag the icon in the Available Icons list box to the position just below the icon that will appear to its left when the set is displayed.

5. To remove an icon from the set, drag the icon in the list box below the name of the SmartIcon set out of the list box.

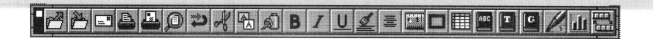

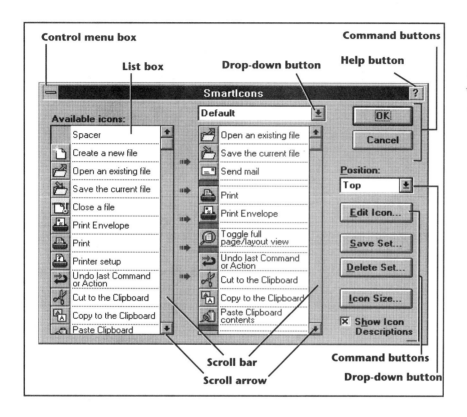

FIGURE 1.3

*Select Tools ➤
SmartIcons when you
want to customize the
SmartIcons in one of
the SmartSuite
applications.*

6. Click on the Save Set command button to display the Save
SmartIcon Set dialog box, similar to that in Figure 1.4.

7. To save the customized SmartIcon set, just click on OK. To create a new set, type a name for the set in the Name Of SmartIcon
Set text box and then click on OK.

8. Click on OK again to close the SmartIcons dialog box.

Save Set of SmartIcons

Name of set:

File name:

Directory: c:\amipro\icons

Current sets:
bonuspac.smi
editing.smi
goodies.smi
graphics.smi
long.smi

OK

Cancel

TIP

To move a button (except in Organizer) on the displayed Smart-Icon set, hold down the Ctrl key while you drag the button to its new position.

Using the Status Bar

Each of the SmartSuite applications except Organizer contains a status bar at the bottom of the screen. The status bar displays information about the current activity and about current settings in the worksheet, document, database, and presentation. Figure 1.5 shows Ami Pro's status bar.

In addition, each status bar contains buttons, such as those labeled in Figure 1.5, which you can use to change the current settings. In Ami Pro, for example, use status bar buttons to change the style applied to a

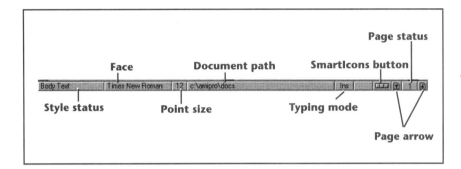

FIGURE 1.5

The status bar displays information about the current file. In addition, you can use buttons on the application's status bar to change some of the settings.

paragraph or the font and size of selected text. As with the SmartIcons, you must have a mouse in order to access the functions of the status bar buttons.

To use one of the status bar buttons, click on it to display a pop-up list of available options. For example, to display a different SmartIcon set, click on the SmartIcons button on the status bar, and then select the name of the set in the pop-up list that appears.

Using Quick Menus

To quickly access a command that does not appear either on the displayed SmartIcon set or the status bar, use the application's quick menus. The quick menus are displayed beside selected data in the application. Quick menus save you from searching for the appropriate command on the menu bar.

The quick menus are really quick. Select the data on which you want to perform a command and then right-click on the selection. A menu appears with commands useful for the specific selection.

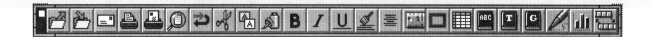

> ### NOTE
>
> **Ami Pro has no quick menus. Instead, the appropriate dialog box appears when you right-click in a specific area of the page rather than on a selection.**

For example, select a range in a 1-2-3 worksheet, and then right-click on the range. The quick menu that appears contains commands to move or copy data, to change the formats applied, and to assign a name to the selection. See Chapter 3 for additional information about these tasks.

Getting Help

If you discover you need help to carry out a command, on-line Help is available in each of the SmartSuite applications. There are several ways to get help:

- Click on the Help button in the upper-right corner of a dialog box to display *context-sensitive* help, or assistance for the options in that dialog box.

- Use ↓ or ↑ to highlight a command on a pull-down or quick menu, and then press Shift+F1 to display the Help window for that command.

- Click on the SuiteAnswers Help button on the SmartCenter SmartIcon set, and then select the type of help you want for SmartSuite.

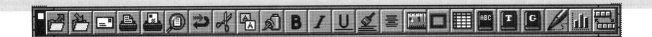

N O T E

You can also access Help by selecting Help ➤ *Command*. The
Help Contents are available on the pull-down menu, as well as
commands used to search for help on a keyword, display
information on how to use Help, and display topics on
keyboard shortcuts and function keys.

Help appears in its own window, which can be manipulated just like
any other window. Figure 1.6 shows the Help window that appears
when you click on the Help button in 1-2-3's SmartIcons dialog box.

Notice that the Help window in Figure 1.6 contains several buttons on its
own button bar. Click on the corresponding button to access the following:

The Contents button displays the list of Help topics for the application.   **Contents**
In 1-2-3, Ami Pro, Freelance Graphics, and Approach, the topics appear
as icons. In Organizer, the topics are underlined. Click on the icon or
underlined topic for which you want help.

The Search button displays the Search dialog box. Type or select a key-   **Search**
word on which you want help, and click on Show Topics. Select the
topic in the list that appears below the list box, and then click on Go To
to display its Help window.

When you click on the Back button, each of the previous Help topics is   **Back**
displayed in turn, starting with the last one.

Click on History to reveal a message box containing a list of Help topics   **History**
you have displayed in this Help session. To return to one of the topics,
double-click on it in the list.

 Click on the Next or Previous button to display the next or previous topic related to the current Help topic.

 When you have finished using Help, double-click on its Control menu box to close the Help window.

FIGURE 1.6

When you request help, a Help window appears with its own button bar.

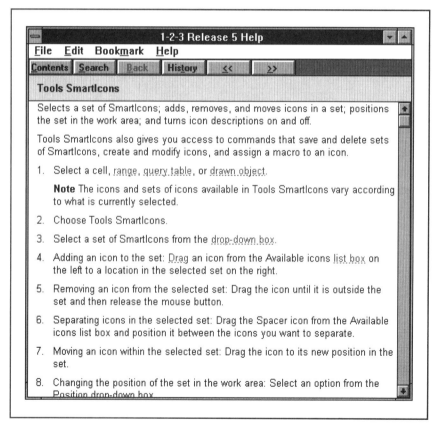

PART TWO

Lotus 1-2-3

CHAPTER TWO

Creating a
Worksheet

CREATING A NEW worksheet is incredibly easy with 1-2-3. You can create a worksheet based on your own design to meet your specific needs, or you can use one of 1-2-3's SmartMasters, which are *templates* (predesigned worksheets) that do almost everything but enter your data.

Starting Lotus 1-2-3

Before you can create your own worksheet, you must start 1-2-3. Follow these steps:

1. Click on the Start Lotus 1-2-3 button on the SmartCenter Smart-Icon set. Select the Don't Show This Screen Again check box. The Welcome to 1-2-3 dialog box, shown in Figure 2.1, appears.

FIGURE 2.1

The Welcome to 1-2-3 dialog box appears each time you start 1-2-3.

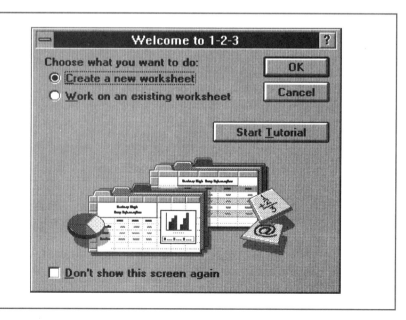

2. Because the Create A New Worksheet option button is already selected, just click on OK. The New File dialog box appears, similar to that in Figure 2.2.

3. The Create A Plain Worksheet check box is already selected, so click on OK to open a new, blank, worksheet similar to that in Figure 2.3.

FIGURE 2.2

The New File dialog box contains a list of SmartMasters you can use to create a worksheet that is already formatted.

New File ?

Create a worksheet by selecting a SmartMaster:

Amortize a Loan
Analyze a Direct Marketing Plan
Analyze Competing Projects
Create a Personal Budget
Create a Territory Sales Plan
Create an Expense Report
Create an Invoice

OK
Cancel
Browse...

X Create a plain worksheet

Comments:

File name:

FIGURE 2.3

When you create a new, blank worksheet, the 1-2-3 window appears.

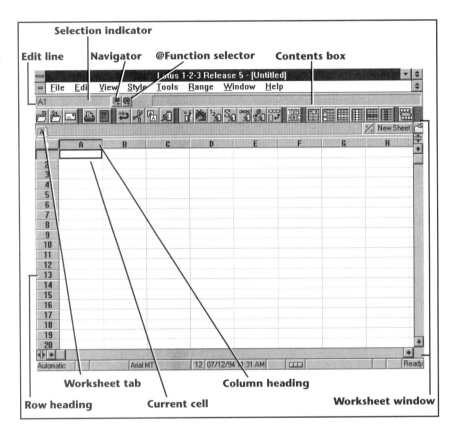

NOTE

To create a new worksheet based on one of the SmartMasters in the New File dialog box, click on the name of the template in the Create A Worksheet By Selecting A SmartMaster list box, and then click on OK. When the SmartMaster appears, click on the icon of the worksheet you want to use.

The 1-2-3 Window

Figure 2.3 shows several important elements of the 1-2-3 user interface. Each labeled element helps you assemble your worksheet:

- The *worksheet window* appears just below the SmartIcons. The worksheet consists of a grid of 256 columns, labeled A, B, C, etc., and 8192 numbered rows. The intersection of a column and a row contains a *cell*. A cell is named (also called the *cell address*) according to its location, using the column letter followed by the row number. For example, the cell in column C and in row 4 is called C4.

- The gray area where the column letter appears is called the *column heading*. The gray area where the row number appears is called the *row heading*.

- The *edit line* appears just below the menu bar and just above the SmartIcons. It contains the *selection indicator*, which displays the current cell or selection, the *Navigator*, used to move to and select a *range* (one or more adjacent cells) to which you have assigned a meaningful name, the *@Function selector*, used to insert an @function into a cell, and the *contents box*, which displays the contents of the current cell.

- The *worksheet tabs*, indicating the worksheets included in the file, appear just above the column headings. For additional information about using multiple worksheets in a file, see Chapter 6.

Entering Data in the Worksheet

To create a worksheet, you must enter meaningful data in the work-sheet's cells. The data you enter is placed in the *current cell*, the cell that is bordered by a heavy black line. To make a cell current (also known as *selecting* the cell), just point to it with your mouse and click the left mouse button. In Figure 2.4, C4 is the current cell.

TIP

As you are entering data in a worksheet, it may be easier to use ↑, ↓, ←, and → to make an adjacent cell current.

Numbers or text, or both numbers and text can be entered in the cur-rent cell. When numbers are entered, 1-2-3 regards them as *values*. Val-ues can be calculated, used in formulas, and used in @functions.

FIGURE 2.4

Point to the cell in which you want to enter data, and then click the left mouse button to make the cell current. In this figure, C4 is the current cell.

	A	B	C	D
1				
2				
3				
4				
5				
6				
7				

N O T E

See Chapter 5 for information about using formulas and @functions to perform calculations.

When text or both text and numbers are entered, 1-2-3 regards them as *labels*. Labels must be preceded by a *label-prefix*, a character that tells 1-2-3 the data is a label instead of a value. However, any time you enter data that begins with a letter, 1-2-3 automatically places the label-prefix, in this case ' (apostrophe), before the characters to indicate that it is a label.

N O T E

Labels that are entered in a cell appear *left-aligned* (aligned along the left edge of the cell) and values are *right-aligned* (aligned along the right edge of the cell) by *default*. A default is a setting that comes with Lotus 1-2-3 when it is installed.

To enter data, type the characters and then press ↵. For example, in the new worksheet you just opened, A1 is selected. If you type **HELLO** and press ↵, "HELLO" appears along the left edge of cell A1.

Follow these steps to begin a sample worksheet:

1. Select cell B1, and then type **North**. As you type, the characters appear in the cell and on the edit line. Press → to enter the data in the cell and select C1.

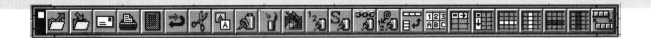

T I P

Use ↑, ↓, ←, and → to simultaneously enter data you have typed and move to an adjacent cell.

---

2. Type **South**, and then press →.

3. Enter **East** in D1 and **West** in E1.

Selecting a Range

Ranges are indicated by the first (top-left) and last (bottom-right) cell addresses. For example, cells C4, C5, C6, D4, D5, and D6 are called C4..D6.

If you select a range, you can manipulate each cell in the range. To select a range, point to the first cell in the range, click and hold down the left mouse button, and then drag the mouse pointer to the last cell in the range and release the button. As you drag, the mouse pointer becomes a dragging pointer. Figure 2.5 shows how C4..D6 appears when it is selected.

Entering a Sequence of Data

One way to use a selected range is to enter a sequence of numbers or data such as the days of the week or the months of the year, into a range of selected cells.

To continue building the sample worksheet using a sequence:

1. Click on the SmartIcons button on the status bar, and then select Editing to display the Editing SmartIcon set.

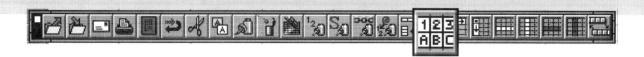

FIGURE 2.5

When you drag to select a range, the mouse pointer changes into a dragging pointer.

2. Select cell A2. Type **January** and press ↵.

3. Select A2..A13, and then click on the Sequence button on the Editing SmartIcon set. Each cell in the range is filled with the name of a month, as shown in Figure 2.6.

To create a sequence with increments greater than one, type data or values in at least two adjacent cells. Then select the two cells along with the range you want to fill with sequential data and click on the Sequence button on the Editing SmartIcon set.

You can also enter sequential data by choosing a command on a selected range's quick menu:

1. Select B2, and then type **894** and press ↵.

2. Select B2..E2, and then click the right mouse button to display the selection's quick menu.

3. Select Fill By Example. The selected cells are filled with 895, 896, and 897.

Fill by Example

FIGURE 2.6

Use the Sequence button to enter a sequence of months in a selected range.

	A	B	C	D	E
1		North	South	East	West
2	January				
3	February				
4	March				
5	April				
6	May				
7	June				
8	July				
9	August				
10	September				
11	October				
12	November				
13	December				
14					

Continue to compile your worksheet by entering numbers. Because most real worksheets are not composed of sequential numbers, just type each number in the corresponding cell and then press ⏎. Your worksheet will resemble that in Figure 2.7.

Saving Data to a File on Your Disk

Once you have entered data you want to keep, save the worksheet to a file on your hard disk. Follow these steps the first time you save a file:

1. Click on the Save button on the Editing SmartIcon set. The Save As dialog box, shown in Figure 2.8, appears.

A	A	B	C	D	E	F
1		North	South	East	West	
2	January	894	895	896	897	
3	February	1027	1083	823	1065	
4	March	561	1245	761	953	
5	April					
6	May					
7	June					
8	July					
9	August					
10	September					
11	October					
12	November					
13	December					
14						

FIGURE 2.7

Enter numbers in cells to complete the first quarter of the sample worksheet.

2. Type the name for your file in the File Name text box. For example, type **SALES** to name the sample worksheet. 1-2-3 automatically adds the .WK4 file extension.

3. If necessary, click in the Comments text box, and then type a description or other information about the file. For example, type **Sample data in a worksheet file**.

4. Click on OK.

OK

FIGURE 2.8

The Save As dialog box appears the first time you save a file. Type the name for your file in the File Name text box. There is no need to type the .WK4 file extension.

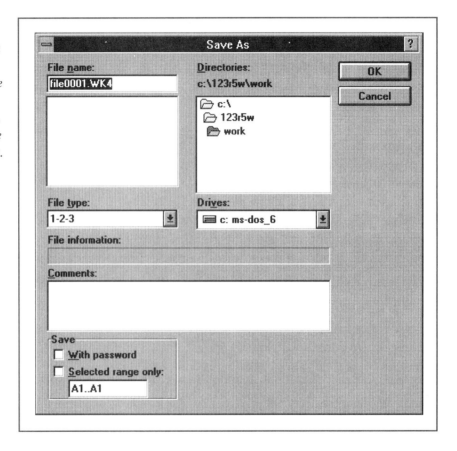

TIP

It is a good idea to save your work often, such as every ten minutes or so, and whenever you take a break from your work. In the event of some calamity (such as a power failure), you will not have to re-enter data that you saved.

When you save a worksheet, it remains on your screen and the file name is displayed in the title bar. You can add more data to the worksheet or edit the data that is already there.

N O T E

See Chapter 3, "Editing Data in the Worksheet," for additional information about adding data or editing existing data.

To save a file that has already been named, just click on the Save button on the Editing SmartIcon set. The file, along with any changes you made to it, is saved to the same file name, so the Save As dialog box does not appear.

To save a file to a new file name, select File ➤ Save As to display the Save As dialog box. Type a new name in the File Name text box, and then click on OK.

Closing the Worksheet File

When you are finished with the current file but want to work some more in 1-2-3, close the file to remove it from your screen and from your computer's memory.

1. Select File ➤ Close.

2. If you made any changes to the worksheet, a dialog box similar to that in Figure 2.9 appears, asking if you want to save your changes.

- Click on Yes to save changes made to the file.

- Click on No to close the file without saving the changes.

- Click on Cancel to keep the worksheet open on your screen.

FIGURE 2.9

Click on Yes to save changes you made to a worksheet before you close it, or No to close the worksheet without saving your changes.

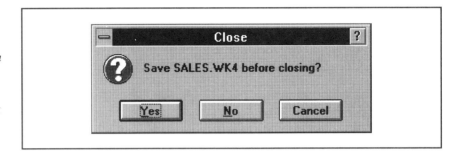

Exiting Lotus 1-2-3

When you have finished your 1-2-3 session, exit Lotus 1-2-3 and return to Windows Program Manager. 1-2-3 automatically displays a dialog box allowing you to save any open files you have changed.

To exit 1-2-3:

1. Double-click on 1-2-3's Control menu box on the left side of the title bar. If you made any changes to an open worksheet or file, the Exit dialog box appears, similar to the Close dialog box in Figure 2.9.

2. Click on one of the buttons, described below.

- Choose Yes to save changes to the active file and close that file. If there is another open file that you have changed since you last saved it, a dialog box appears for that file as well.

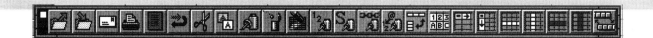

N O T E

If you have not saved a worksheet to a file on your disk, the Save As dialog box appears. Type a name for the file and click on OK.

- Choose No to exit 1-2-3 without saving any changes.

- Choose Cancel to return to your 1-2-3 session without closing any worksheets or files.

- Choose Save All to save the changes to all open files and then close 1-2-3. If you have not previously saved a worksheet to a named file, the Save As dialog box appears.

CHAPTER THREE

Editing Data in
the Worksheet

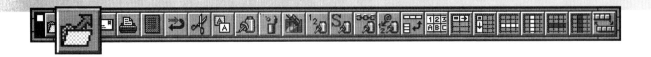

T IS OFTEN necessary to add or correct data in your worksheets. In fact, that is one of the wonderful things about using 1-2-3 to prepare a worksheet—you can insert, move, copy, delete, and add data without having to redo the whole worksheet.

N O T E

Use buttons on the Editing SmartIcon set that you learned about in Chapter 2 to begin working on the examples in this chapter.

Opening a File on Your Disk

Once a worksheet is saved to a file on your disk, you can open the file to make changes or additions to it. Several files can be open simultaneously, depending on the amount of memory in your computer.

1. Click on the Start 1-2-3 button on the SmartCenter SmartIcon set.

2. Click on the Open button on the Editing SmartIcon set. The Open File dialog box, similar to that in Figure 3.1, appears.

3. Double-click on SALES.WK4 in the File Name list box.

When you open a file, it appears just as it did when you last saved it. Even the cell that was selected when you saved the file is the current cell when you open the file.

FIGURE 3.1

Click on the Open button or choose File ➤ Open (Ctrl+O) to display the Open File dialog box.

Open File	?

File name:
`*.wk*`

sales.wk4

Directories:
c:\lotsuite\123r5w\work

c:\
lotsuite
123r5w
work

OK
Cancel
Combine

File type:
1-2-3 (wk*)

Drives:
c: ms-dos_6

File information:

Comments:

TIP

The last five files that were open are listed at the bottom of the File pull-down menu. To open one of them, click on File to pull down the File menu, and then select *Filename*.

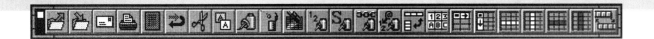

Opening a New File

Sometimes you will need to open a new file while working in 1-2-3. Follow these steps to open a new, blank file:

1. Select File ➤ New. The New File dialog box appears.

2. If necessary, select the Create A Plain Worksheet check box.

3. Click on OK to open a new worksheet.

OK

1-2-3 automatically assigns a file name, which appears in the title bar, to the worksheet. However, you can change the name of the file when you save the worksheet for the first time.

Changing Existing Data

Any time you make a change to a worksheet, such as moving, copying, inserting, replacing, and deleting data, you are *editing* the worksheet. You can only edit the contents of the current cell. Use buttons on the Editing SmartIcon set to easily perform some of your edits.

Moving and Copying Data

There are several ways to move or copy selected data. Two of the quickest ways are to use your mouse and either cut, copy, and paste, or drag and drop a selection.

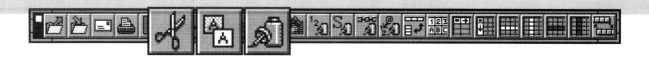

Using Cut, Copy, and Paste

The Cut, Copy, and Paste commands are available in virtually every
Windows application. The Cut and Copy commands place selected data
in the Windows Clipboard, where it stays until it is replaced by new
data that you cut or copy to the Clipboard. In 1-2-3, the Paste command places a copy of the Clipboard's contents in the selected cell or
range.

To move data, select the cell or range that contains the data and then
click on the Cut button on the Editing SmartIcon set. The selection is removed from the worksheet, and a copy is placed in the Clipboard.

To copy data, select the cell or range that contains the data you want to
copy, and then click on the Copy button. The selection remains in the
worksheet, and a copy is placed in the Clipboard.

WARNING

Each time you cut or copy a selection to the Clipboard, it replaces the current contents of the Clipboard.

The Clipboard contents can be pasted as many times as you wish. To
paste the contents of the Clipboard, select the cell or range in which
you want to place a copy of the Clipboard contents, and then click on
the Paste button on the Editing SmartIcon set.

Using Drag and Drop

Using drag and drop is the quickest and easiest way to move or copy data from one location to another on your screen. However, with drag and drop you bypass the Clipboard, so you cannot paste data into multiple locations.

To use drag and drop, follow these steps:

1. Select the data you want to move or copy.

2. Move the mouse pointer near the edge of the selection until it appears as a hand.

3. To move the selection, click and hold down the left mouse button. The hand changes into a fist (pretty clever) with a cell attached to indicate the selection has been "grabbed." Drag the selection to a different location. As you drag, an outline of the selection appears on the worksheet. When the outline surrounds the range in which you want the data to appear, release the mouse button to drop the selection.

4. To copy the selection, press the Ctrl key while you drag. The fist appears with a plus sign in it.

Editing Data in a Cell

Often, you will want to replace or add to data that you have entered in worksheet cells.

To replace the current contents of the selected cell, simply type the data and then press ↵. This is the same method you used to enter data in an empty cell.

To insert data in a non-blank cell, select the cell, and then click in the contents box on the edit line to activate it. When the contents box is active, you can add characters at the location of the insertion point. Follow these steps to activate the contents box in the SALES.WK4 worksheet:

1. Select Window ➤ SALES.WK4.

2. Select A2, and then click anywhere in the contents box.

> **NOTE**
>
> **To edit the contents of a cell directly in the cell, double-click on the cell. Then insert or delete the necessary characters using the same methods as for editing in the contents box.**

If the insertion point is not located where you want to insert characters, move the mouse pointer, which appears in the contents box as an

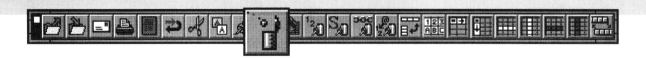

I-beam, to the desired position and click. For example, move the mouse pointer between the u and the a and click.

Then just type the characters you want to insert. For example, press the spacebar, and then type **This is a test**. The characters you type appear both in the contents box and in the current cell.

When all the characters you want appear in the active contents box, click on the Confirm box to the left of the contents box to enter the edited data into the current cell.

However, if you want to cancel all the changes you made in the contents box, as with this example, click on the Cancel box while the contents box is active.

Deleting Data

Use any of the following methods to delete data in a worksheet:

- To delete the contents of a selected cell or range, click on the Delete button on the Editing SmartIcon set.

- To delete one character in a cell, double-click on the cell, and then click to the right of the character to be deleted and press Backspace, or to the left of the character and press Del. Click on the Confirm box beside the contents box to enter the changes you made.

- To delete several characters, double-click in the cell, highlight the characters to be deleted, press either Del or Backspace, and then click on the Confirm box by the contents box.

- To simultaneously delete characters and replace them with others, double-click on the cell you want to edit, highlight the characters to be replaced, type the new characters, and then click on the Confirm box.

Using Undo

If you accidentally edit the contents of a cell, you can click immediately on the Undo button on the Editing SmartIcon set to reverse your last command or action.

For example, select A2 in SALES.WK4 and click on the Delete button. Now click on the Undo button to return the data to the cells.

Go ahead and save the worksheet now. We will use it to practice formatting techniques in Chapter 4.

Moving through Worksheet Data

So far, you've been using only the portion of the worksheet that currently appears on your screen. However, the worksheet is much larger than what is displayed. You must display whatever portion of the worksheet you wish to edit.

Scrolling through a Worksheet

Use your mouse and the scroll bars to display a different portion of a worksheet.

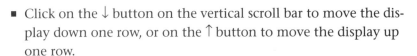

> **NOTE**
>
> When you scroll through a worksheet, the current cell or range does not change. To move the insertion point to a different cell, click on the cell after you scroll.

To move the display up or down:

- Click on the ↓ button on the vertical scroll bar to move the display down one row, or on the ↑ button to move the display up one row.

- Drag the scroll box up or down to display a general vertical portion of the worksheet.

- Click on the scroll bar above the scroll box to move the display up one screen. Click below the scroll box to move down one screen.

To move the display left or right:

- Click on the → button on the horizontal scroll bar to display the next column, or on the ← button to display the previous column.

- Drag the scroll box to display a general horizontal portion of the worksheet.

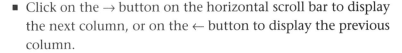

- Click to the left of the scroll box to display one screen left, or to the right of the scroll box to display one screen right.

T I P

To move the display to the beginning of the worksheet, press Ctrl+Home.

Moving to a Named Range

Another easy way to move around a worksheet is to move to a named range. Use 1-2-3's Navigator to simultaneously move to and select a named range in a worksheet. Before you can use Navigator, you must name a range in your worksheet.

Naming a Range

Range names are used instead of cell addresses. Often it is convenient to assign a meaningful name to a range of data so you can use the name in a formula, move to and select it, or print a specific range.

There are several rules to remember when naming ranges:

- Range names can contain up to 15 uppercase or lowercase characters.

- Range names can contain a number, a - (hyphen), and an ! (exclamation point). However, do not *begin* a name with any of these characters.

- Do not use any of the following characters in a range name: space, , (comma), ; (semicolon), . (period), + (plus sign), – (minus sign), * (asterisk), / (slash), & (ampersand), > (greater than sign), < (less than sign), @ (at sign), # (pound sign), or { (brace).

Let's name a range in the SALES.WK4 worksheet:

1. Select B2..B13.

2. Right-click on the selection to display the quick menu.

Name...

3. Select Name. The Name dialog box, shown in Figure 3.2, appears.

FIGURE 3.2

Use a selection's quick menu to choose Name when you want to name the range in a worksheet.

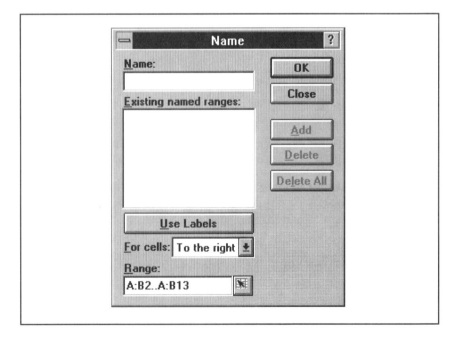

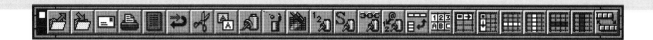

4. Type **North** in the Name text box.

5. Click on OK to name the selected range. Then click on another cell anywhere in the worksheet to deselect the range.

Using Navigator

Use Navigator to move to and select the range named North.

1. Click on Navigator on the edit line to display a list of all the named ranges in the worksheet.

2. Select NORTH. Navigator selects B2..B13.

Using Navigator to move to and select a named range is particularly useful in a large worksheet. You can move or copy the selected range as described earlier in this chapter.

Formatting Your Worksheet and Data

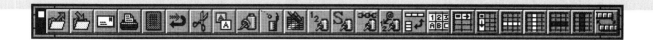

THERE ARE TWO ways to enhance the appearance of a worksheet. You can change either the *format* (appearance) of the data or change the format of the actual worksheet. Most often, you must do both to create a professional-looking worksheet.

Formatting the data includes applying attributes (such as boldface or italics), changing the font and size of the characters, and applying a number format to values in the worksheet. Formatting the worksheet includes adding borders and colors to a selection, changing the row height and the column width, and freezing a row or column of labels so it always appears on your screen. This chapter discusses all of these techniques.

Formatting Data in a Worksheet

You can easily change the appearance of worksheet data from 1-2-3's default formats. Use the Formatting SmartIcon set buttons and the status bar buttons to enhance, align, and change the format of numbers or the font in a selected cell or range.

Aligning Data in a Cell

By default, labels are left-aligned within cells and numbers are right-aligned. However, you can change the alignment of data in selected cells. Changing the alignment of labels often makes it easier to read worksheet data.

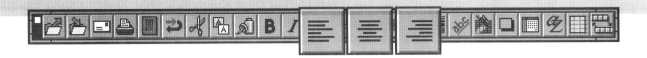

To realign the data in the SALES.WK4 worksheet:

1. Click on the Next Set Of SmartIcons button on the Editing SmartIcon set to display the Formatting SmartIcon set.

2. To center the labels in B1..E1, select B1..E1 and then click on the Center button on the Formatting SmartIcon set.

3. Now select A2..A13 and click on the Align Right button to align each label along the right edge of its cell. Glance at the contents box to see that right-aligned labels appear with a " (quotation mark) in front of the characters.

NOTE

To align data in the current cell along the left edge of the cell (the default), click on the Align Left button.

Aligning Data across Cells in Several Columns

To further enhance a worksheet, you can change the alignment of data in one cell so it is spaced across cells selected in several columns of the same row.

1. Select the cell containing the data you want to realign as the first (left-most) cell, and then select cells in the same row adjacent to the first cell, as shown here:

Alignment...

2. Right-click on the selection, and then select Alignment in the quick menu that appears. The Alignment dialog box, shown in Figure 4.1, appears.

3. In the Horizontal area, click on the Center option button to center the data within the selection, or the Evenly Spaced option button to position the data evenly throughout the selection.

FIGURE 4.1

Select the Across Columns check box and either the Center or the Evenly Spaced option button to align the data across several columns.

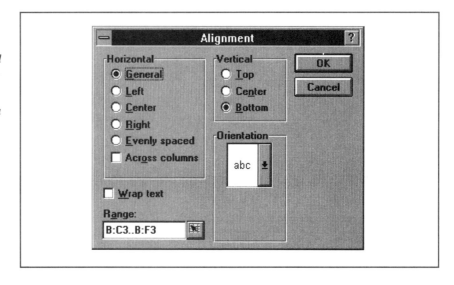

4. Select the Across Columns check box.

5. Click on OK.

OK

N O T E

Even though the data appears to be in several cells, it is actually still in the first cell you selected.

Changing the Font and Size

Characters entered into a worksheet appear by default in the Arial MT *font,* or typeface, in 12-point size. Use the Font and Point Size buttons on the status bar to choose a different typeface and size for selected cells.

1. Select B1..E1.

2. Click on the Font button on the status bar to display a pop-up list of available fonts. Scroll down the list until Times New Roman is displayed, and then select it.

Arial MT

3. Now click on the Point Size button on the status bar to display a pop-up list of available point sizes for the Times New Roman font. Select 18 in the list.

Applying Attributes to Selected Data

To further enhance the appearance of the worksheet, add attributes to the column and row labels. More than one attribute can be applied to the data in selected cells.

- If necessary, select B1..E1. Click on the Bold button on the Formatting SmartIcon set to apply bold format to the characters in each cell. Then click on the Underline button to underline each label.

- Select A2..A13 and click on the Bold button to apply bold format. Now click on the Italics button to also apply italics to the data.

Changing the Number Format

By default, numbers are assigned the Automatic number format, which means 1-2-3 will automatically display numbers depending on the way they were entered. For example, to have 1-2-3 automatically display numbers as currency, type $ (dollar sign) before the number, and then press ↵. To have 1-2-3 automatically display numbers as a percentage, enter the number followed by the % (percent sign).

The numbers in the sample worksheet were entered without assigning a format. Follow these steps to change the numbers in B2..E4 to appear as currency:

1. Select B2..E4.

2. Click on the Number Format button on the status bar to display a pop-up list of number formats.

3. Select US Dollar in the list. Your worksheet should appear similar to that in Figure 4.2.

	A	B	C	D	E	F
1		**North**	**South**	**East**	**West**	
2	*January*	$894.00	$895.00	$896.00	$897.00	
3	*February*	$1,027.00	$1,083.00	$823.00	$1,065.00	
4	*March*	$561.00	$1,245.00	$761.00	$953.00	
5	*April*					
6	*May*					
7	*June*					
8	*July*					
9	*August*					
10	*eptember*					
11	*October*					
12	*Vovember*					
13	*December*					
14						

FIGURE 4.2

It is easy to change the appearance of data in selected cells using the alignment and attribute buttons on the Formatting SmartIcon set, and the Number Format, Font, and Point Size buttons on the status bar. The values in the selected range were changed by choosing US Dollar in the Number Format pop-up list.

There are many different number formats available in the pop-up list that appears when you click on the Number Format button on the status bar.

Automatic

- Choose from a variety of formats in which to display dates and times.

- Select Fixed to change numbers so that a specific number (from 0 to 15) of decimal places is displayed. If necessary, click on the Decimal Places button on the status bar to display a pop-up list, and then select the number of decimal places to display.

- Select Scientific to display numbers in exponential notation.

- To display numbers with comma signs as thousand separators, select Comma.

- Select General to display numbers with no thousand separators, a minus sign for negative numbers, and no trailing 0 after the decimal point.

- To change numbers in selected cells to labels, select Label.

- To display formulas instead of their results in selected cells, select Text.

- To change numbers in selected cells to percentages, select Percent. The numbers are multiplied by 100 and the % (percent sign) appears after each.

Copying Formats to a Range

As you have seen, you can apply various formats to the same data. All the formats that have been applied to specific data are called the *style* of the data. You can easily copy or remove styles from worksheet data.

NOTE

Styles include the number format, font and size, attributes, alignment, the colors, patterns, and borders applied, and the protection setting.

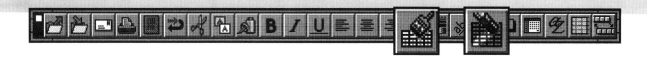

1. In the SALES.WK4 worksheet, enter **Monthly Total** in F1.

> **NOTE**
>
> There are too many characters in F1, so some of them appear
> to be in G1. However, they are really in F1. You can see this if
> you enter data in G1. The characters in F1 that spilled over into
> G1 seem to disappear altogether.

2. Select E1, and then click on the Fast Format button on the Formatting SmartIcon set.

3. Click on F1 to copy all the formats that were applied to E1. Then click on the Fast Format button again to toggle it off.

To delete the style applied to a selected range, click on the Delete Styles button on the Formatting SmartIcon set.

Formatting a Worksheet

As you continue to build the SALES.WK4 worksheet, you can see that some changes should be made to the structure of the worksheet. For example, column A must be widened so some of the characters are not cut off, and column F must be widened so the characters in F1 do not spill into G1.

> **NOTE**
>
> If a value entered in a cell is too wide, 1-2-3 displays it either in
> scientific notation or with asterisks across the cell.

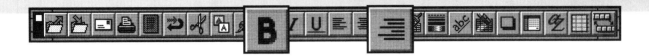

To make using the worksheet easier, you can freeze the descriptive labels on the screen. You can also enhance the appearance of the worksheet by adding borders and colors.

Changing the
Row Height and Column Width

Changing the height of a row or the width of a column is a breeze. Using your mouse, you can change the row height and column width to either a general or a specific measurement. In the following steps, use the SALES.WK4 worksheet as an example.

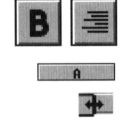

1. Enter **Division Total** in A15, and then click on the Bold and Align Right buttons on the Formatting SmartIcon set.

2. To change the width of column A to a general measurement (the eyeball method), point to the column heading and then move the mouse pointer to the right edge of its border. When the pointer changes into a two-headed arrow intersected by a vertical line, drag the edge of the column to the right to increase the column width.

NOTE

To decrease the width of a column, drag the right edge of the column heading to the left.

3. To assign a specific measurement to column F, click on the column heading to select the entire column. Then right-click on

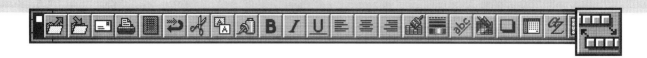

the selection and choose Column Width in the quick menu. The Column Width dialog box, shown in Figure 4.3, appears.

Column Width...

FIGURE 4.3

Use the Column Width dialog box when you want to specify the exact width of a column in characters.

4. Click and hold the ↑ spin wheel button until 16 appears in the Set Width To Characters text box.

5. Click on OK to change the width of column F.

TIP

To have 1-2-3 automatically adjust the width of a column, click on the Next Set button on the Formatting SmartIcon set to display the Goodies SmartIcon set. Then select a cell in the column and click on the Column Width button. The width of the column is adjusted to accommodate the widest entry in the column.

6. To change the height of row 17 by dragging, move the mouse pointer to the lower edge of the row heading. The mouse

pointer changes into a two-headed arrow intersected by a horizontal line. Drag the mouse pointer up to decrease the height of the row or down to increase the height of the row.

T I P

By default, 1-2-3 adjusts the row height to fit the height of the largest font in the row. To return the row height of a manually changed row to the default, double-click on the row heading's lower border.

Row Height...

7. To assign a specific height to row 15, click on its row heading to select the entire row, and then right-click on the selection. Select Row Height in the quick menu to display the Row Height dialog box, shown in Figure 4.4.

8. Click on the Set Height To Points option button, and then click and hold down the ↑ spin wheel button until 20 appears in the text box.

OK

9. Click on OK to change the height of row 15.

FIGURE 4.4

Select Row Height from the quick menu when you want to specify the exact height of a row in points.

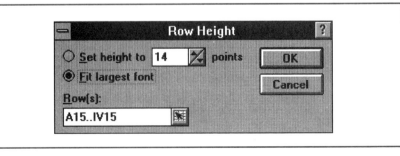

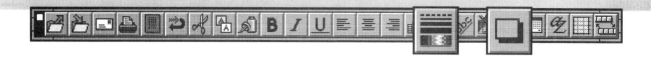

Adding Lines, Borders, and Colors to a Range

To further enhance the appearance of the worksheet, add borders and colors to it.

1. Click on the SmartIcons button on the status bar, and then select Formatting in the pop-up list to display the Formatting SmartIcons.

2. Select A15..F15.

3. Click on the Lines, Borders, and Colors button on the Formatting SmartIcon set to display the Lines & Color dialog box, shown in Figure 4.5.

4. Click on the Background Color drop-down button to display a color palette, and then click on one of the colors in the palette.

5. In the Border area of the dialog box, select the Top check box to add a line (border) to the top of the selection.

6. Click on the Line Style drop-down button, and then select the double line displayed in the list.

7. Click on OK in the Lines & Color dialog box.

TIP

To add a drop shadow border to a selected range, click on the **Drop Shadow** button on the Formatting SmartIcon set.

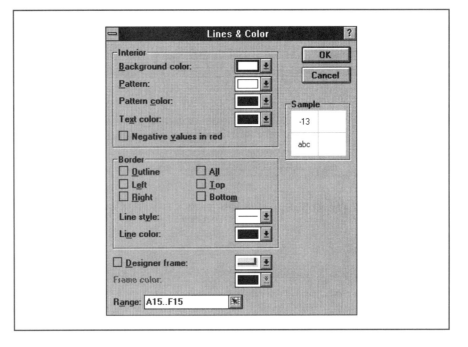

Inserting a Row or Column

Use buttons on the Editing SmartIcon set to quickly insert or delete a row or column in a worksheet.

1. Click on the SmartIcons button on the status bar, and then click on Editing in the pop-up list to switch to the Editing SmartIcon set.

2. Select A1..A3, and then click on the Insert Rows button on the Editing SmartIcon set. Because cells in three rows were selected, three rows were inserted above the selected cells.

3. Select any cell in column B, and then click on the Insert Columns button. Because you selected a cell in only one column, only one column was inserted in the location of the selection.

Freezing a Row or Column on a Worksheet

As you scroll through a large worksheet, it is easy to forget which column contains what data. You can freeze the display of the column and/or row labels, called *worksheet titles*, on your screen.

1. Select B5, and then choose View ➤ Freeze Titles. The Freeze Titles dialog box, shown in Figure 4.6, appears.

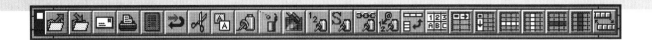

FIGURE 4.6

Select View ➤ Freeze Titles when you want to freeze rows above or to the left of the selected cell.

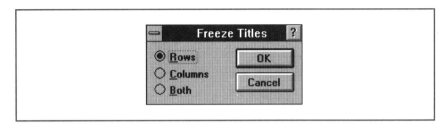

2. Click on the Both option button to freeze rows 1 through 4 and column A.

3. Click on OK.

NOTE

In step 2 above, select the Rows option button to freeze only the rows above the selected cell, or the Columns option button to freeze only the columns to the left of the selected cell.

If you scroll down through the worksheet, you can see that rows 1 through 4 stay at the top of the display. If you scroll to the right, you'll see that column A remains displayed. Press Ctrl+Home to return to the beginning of the worksheet.

Performing Calculations on Your Data

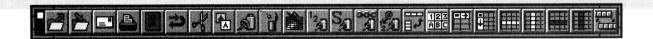

THE PRIMARY USE for a worksheet is to calculate values entered in its cells. In 1-2-3, formulas are the means used to perform the calculations. You can create your own formulas or use the @functions, the formulas that are included in 1-2-3.

Using Formulas

A formula is a mathematical calculation, created using the same rules you learned in elementary school. 1-2-3 automatically performs the calculations specified in a formula entered in a worksheet cell and displays the *results* (the answer) of the formula in the same cell. The actual formula appears in the contents box when the cell is current.

N O T E

The results of a calculation appear in the number format assigned to the cell that contains the formula.

Elements of a Formula

Several components are used to make up a formula:

- A formula contains values, also called *operands*, that are either numbers or text. Numbers, cell addresses, or range names can be used as the operands in a formula.

- *Operators* (mathematical symbols) are used to perform calculations on the operands. The formula is calculated from left to right, but the operations are performed using 1-2-3's order of

precedence. Table 5.1 shows the order in which operations are performed.

- *Separators* are used to prioritize operations within a complex formula. For example, use ( ) (parentheses) to indicate which portion of a complex formula is to be calculated first. In formulas with several sets of parentheses, the calculations within the innermost parentheses are performed first.

Operator	Function
^	Exponentiation
+ or −	Positive or negative value
* and /	Multiplication and division
+ and −	Addition and subtraction
= or < >	Equal to or not equal to
< or >	Less than or greater than
<=	Less than or equal to
>=	Greater than or equal to
#NOT#	Logical operator NOT
#AND# and #OR#	Logical operators AND and OR
&	Text linking

TABLE 5.1

Order of Precedence for Operators

Entering a Formula in the Worksheet

There are several different ways to enter a formula. Often, you will use a combination of the following methods to enter formulas in a worksheet.

Entering a Simple Formula

To enter a simple formula that contains only numeric values, just type the formula in the current cell and press ↵.

1. Open a new, blank worksheet file.

2. Enter **4** in A1 and **8** in B1.

3. Select C1, and then type **4+8** and press ↵.

Notice that the contents of C1 appear as the results of the formula, in this case, 12. However, look at the contents box on the edit line while C1 is still selected to see the formula that produced the value in C1.

TIP

To display and print the formulas instead of their results in selected worksheet cells, click on the Number Format button on the status bar, and then click on Text in the pop-up list.

Entering a Formula Using Your Mouse

To enter a formula with a cell address as the first value, always begin the formula with + (plus sign), – (minus sign), or = (equal to sign) to tell 1-2-3

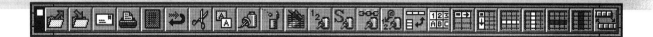

that you are entering a formula. Then either type the cell address or click on the cell after you have typed an operator.

1. Select C4, and then type +.

2. Click on the cell that contains the first value, A1.

3. Type + to tell 1-2-3 you want to add the next value.

4. Click on B1 to place the second operand in the formula.

5. Type +, and then click on C1. The formula appears as +A:A1+A:B1+A:C1 in both the cell and the contents box.

NOTE

See Chapter 6, "Using Multiple Worksheets," for an explanation of the *A:* that appears before each cell address while you are entering the formula.

6. Click on the Confirm box to enter the formula in C4.

Entering More Complex Formulas

When working with complex formulas, add separators to tell 1-2-3 how to prioritize the operations.

1. Select B7.

2. Enter **(100/(C1-B1))*C4**. Use both the typing and selecting methods to enter the formula.

1-2-3 calculates the formula in the following order: (C1–B1) =4; 100/4=25; 25*24=600. If you remove the separators, the operations are performed in a different order. 1-2-3 starts on the left using the default order of precedence. The first operation is 100/C1 = 8.333 and the second operation is –B1*C4= –192, so the result of +8.333 –192 is –183.667.

Moving and Copying Formulas

Formulas can be moved and copied using either the Cut, Copy, and Paste buttons on the Editing SmartIcon set or drag and drop. (See Chapter 3 if you need a reminder on how to move or copy data.) However, before you move or copy a formula, you should understand how moving a formula affects the *references* (cell addresses or range names) to values.

Relative, Absolute, and Mixed References

You can assign a reference type to a cell address in a formula in order to designate how 1-2-3 calculates the formula if it is moved or copied to a different location.

- By default, references to cells in formulas are *relative references*, which means the cell references are automatically adjusted in relation to their new location. For example, copy the formula in B7 to B8. The result appears as ERR in the cell. Glance at the contents box to see that the formula in B8 is (100/(C2–B2))*C5. The cell references have been adjusted to the cells below those in the original formula because the formula was copied to the cell below its original location.

- *Absolute references* always refer to a specific cell address. To change a relative reference to an absolute reference, place a $ before the column letter and before the row number in the cell address. For example, edit the formula in B7 so that it appears as 100/(C1–B1)*C4. If you move or copy the formula to another cell, you will see the same formula and the same results as in B7.

- A cell address in a formula can also contain both a relative and absolute reference, called a *mixed reference*. In a mixed reference, part of the cell address is relative and the other part is absolute. For example, to always refer to a value in column C relative to row 1, the cell address appears as $C1. To refer to a value relative to column C but always in row 1, the cell address is entered as C$1.

Moving a Formula or Its Data

Moving either a formula or the data in cells that are referenced in the formula also affects the formula. To demonstrate:

1. Enter **A1*B1** in B10. Move the formula to B11, and then glance at the contents box to see that it still appears as A1*B1. If you move only the formula, the cell references in it stay the same.

2. Move A1..B1 to A9..B9, and then select B11 and look at the contents box. If you move only the data referred to in a formula, the cell references to the data are adjusted in the formula.

3. Edit the formula in B11 so the cell references are absolute. Then select A9..B11 and move the selection to F9..G11. Select G11 and glance at the contents box to see that even absolute references are adjusted when you move both a formula and its references.

Using @Functions

1-2-3 comes with more than 200 built-in formulas, called @functions, that are useful for performing a variety of specific calculations. Use the @functions along with your own formulas to calculate values in a worksheet.

A complex formula can be composed of both @functions and your own formulas.

An @function is composed of three parts:

- It always begins with @ (at sign).
- The name of the function appears just after the @.
- The @function's *arguments* appear in parentheses after its name, separated by commas. An argument is the value used to calculate the @function. Just as in the formulas you create, an argument can be a number, text, a cell address, or a range.

NOTE

Almost all the @functions have at least one argument. However, there are some that don't require any arguments, such as @NOW, which returns the date and time set in your computer, and @RAND, which returns a random number between 0 and 1.

@Function Categories

The @functions are divided into ten categories of specialized formulas, making it easy to choose the appropriate @function for the particular job at hand. 1-2-3 includes @functions that perform calculations on dates and times, text, and investments, as well as @functions to perform regular mathematical calculations.

To display a list of the @functions within each category, select Help ➤ Contents, and then click on the @Functions icon in the Help window. Select @Function Categories in the list of topics that appears, and then select the category of @functions you want to see.

- Use *Calendar* @functions to calculate both dates and times.

- Use *Database* @functions to query or perform calculations on data in a database table created in 1-2-3.

- Use *Engineering* @functions to perform engineering computations and calculate advanced mathematical procedures.

- Use *Financial* @functions to perform calculations that define depreciation and cash flows, provide an analysis of investments, and determine loan payments.

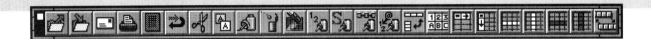

- Use @functions in the *Information* category to provide information about the worksheet or operating system, or to label cells with incorrect or missing information.

- Use *Logical* @functions to provide results of *logical formulas* (formulas that require a true or false answer).

- Use *Lookup* @functions to return the contents of a specified cell or range.

- Use *Mathematical* @functions to calculate a wide variety of mathematical procedures. Everything from trigonometric functions to finding the square root of a value is included in this category.

- Use *Statistical* @functions to calculate listed values, such as finding the minimum, maximum, average, or sum of the values in a list.

- Use *Text* @functions to manipulate text in a selected range.

Using an @Function

Just as with formulas you create, @functions can be entered into a worksheet in a couple of ways. Either type the @function into a cell (the hard way), or use 1-2-3's @function selector (the easy way).

If you type the @function into a worksheet cell, you must correctly enter the name of the function, the separators, and the arguments in the correct order. Instead, use the @function selector to take the hassle out of using @functions.

1. Open the SALES.WK4 worksheet.

2. To remove the empty column B, select any cell in the column, and then click on the Delete Columns button on the Editing SmartIcon set.

3. Now select B18.

4. Click on the @function selector on the edit line, and then select List all. The @Function List dialog box, shown in Figure 5.1, appears.

5. Type **S** to quickly scroll through the list to the first @function that begins with S. A description of the highlighted function appears in the area below the @Functions list box.

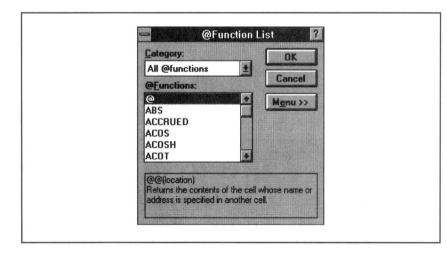

FIGURE 5.1

An alphabetical list of all of 1-2-3's @functions appears in the @Function List dialog box.

To display an alphabetized list of @functions in a specific category, click on the Category drop-down list button, and then select the name of the category. If necessary, scroll through the drop-down list to find the category you want.

6. Scroll through the list until SUM appears, and then select SUM.

7. Click on OK to enter the @function's name and the argument it requires in B18. The argument (list) is already highlighted so you can replace it with the worksheet range to be used as the list to total.

8. Drag through B5..B16 to select the range for the argument.

9. Click on the Confirm box to enter the @function and its correct argument in B18. The results of the @function appear in the cell, and the @function appears in the contents box.

You probably noticed that some of the most useful @functions were displayed in the pop-up list that appeared when you clicked the @function selector. Select one of those functions to use as a shortcut, bypassing the @Function List dialog box.

1. Select C18, and then click the @function selector.

2. Select SUM in the @function selector pop-up list. The @function appears in C18 with its argument already selected.

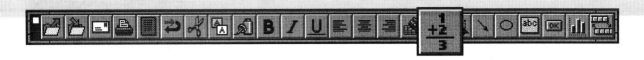

3. Drag through C5..C16 to replace the argument with the range to be totaled.

4. Click on the Confirm box.

T I P

To automatically add the values in the column above a selected cell or the row to the left of a selected cell, click on the SUM button on the Default Sheet SmartIcon set.

CHAPTER SIX

Working with Multiple–Worksheet Files

ONE OF 1-2-3's most useful features is that you can work with files that contain more than one worksheet (*multiple-worksheet files*), to keep worksheets with related but distinct data in the same file. For example, you can keep monthly sales data on one worksheet, and quarterly sales data on another in the same file.

Using multiple-worksheet files to manipulate your data can save a lot of time, because all the data related to a specific topic can be stored in one file and accessed with a click of your mouse.

Inserting a New Worksheet

Each 1-2-3 file originally contains one worksheet. However, you can insert up to 255 additional worksheets in each file, depending on the amount of data in each worksheet and the amount of memory in your computer. Look at the worksheet tabs, which appear just above the column headings shown in Figure 6.1, to see if the current file contains multiple worksheets.

1-2-3 automatically assigns each worksheet tab a letter of the alphabet. The original worksheet is labeled A, and subsequent worksheets are labeled B, C, D, etc. To enter or edit data in one of the worksheets in a multiple-worksheet file, first click on its tab to make it the *current worksheet*—the worksheet that contains the current cell.

Notice in Figure 6.1 that there are also several buttons on the worksheet tabs line. Use the following buttons to manipulate your worksheets:

- Click on the *New Sheet* button to insert a new worksheet in a file.

- Click on the *Hide or Show Tabs* button to *toggle* (turn off and on) the display of worksheet tabs. Click the button first to hide displayed tabs. Click it again to display the hidden worksheet tabs.

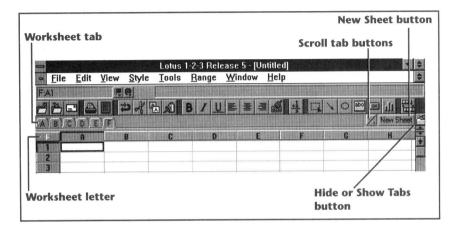

FIGURE 6.1

A multiple-worksheet file displays the tabs that represent each individual worksheet in the file.

- Click on the *worksheet letter*, located on the line below the worksheet tabs just to the left of the column headings, to select the current worksheet.

- Click on the *Scroll Tabs* button to scroll the displayed worksheet tabs to the left or right.

Inserting One Worksheet

The easiest way to add a worksheet to a file is to click on the New Sheet button on the worksheet tabs line. The new worksheet is inserted after the current worksheet.

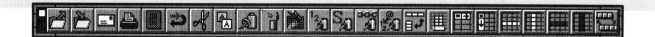

N O T E

When you insert a new worksheet after the current worksheet and before the next worksheet in a file, all the letters on the worksheet tabs after the current worksheet are automatically changed.

You can also simultaneously select the entire worksheet and use its quick menu to insert a new worksheet.

F

1. Right-click on the tab of the worksheet you want to select. Or, right-click on the current worksheet's worksheet letter. The worksheet is selected and its quick menu appears.

Insert...

2. Select Insert to insert a new worksheet.

N O T E

The letter of the current worksheet appears in the contents box on the edit line along with the current cell. For example, if the contents box contains G:C12, the current cell is C12 in worksheet G.

Inserting Several Worksheets

You can also add worksheets either before or after the current worksheet and simultaneously insert several worksheets in a file.

1. Click on the tab of the worksheet where you want to insert additional worksheets.

2. Select Edit ➤ Insert (Ctrl++). The Insert dialog box, shown in Figure 6.2, appears.

3. Click on the Sheet option button. The Insert dialog box changes, as shown in Figure 6.3.

4. Choose the Before or After option button to insert the worksheet(s) before or after the current worksheet.

5. Click on the arrow buttons in the Quantity text box to increase (↑) or decrease (↓) the number of worksheets to be inserted.

6. Click on OK to insert the worksheets.

FIGURE 6.2

To insert several worksheets before or after the current worksheet, select Edit ➤ Insert to display the Insert dialog box.

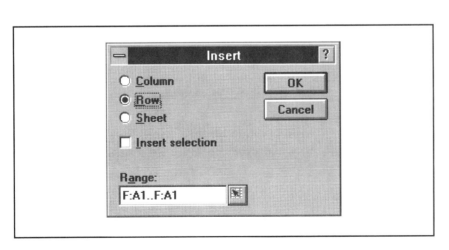

FIGURE 6.3

When Sheet is selected as the Insert option, the Insert dialog box changes so you can choose the position and number of worksheets to add.

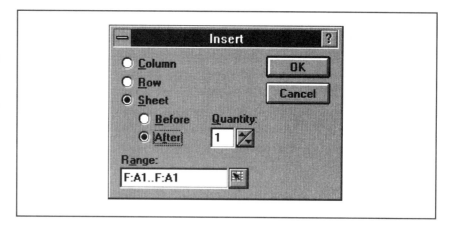

Selecting Ranges in Multiple Worksheets

To edit or format the data in multiple worksheets or ranges in a file, you must first select them.

For example, to change the format or apply attributes to data in the same range but in adjacent worksheets, select a *3D range* (a range that spans multiple adjacent worksheets in a file).

WARNING

Any command or action you perform to a selection takes place in the entire selection. For example, if you select a 3D range and then click on the Delete button on the Editing SmartIcon set, all the data in the 3D range is deleted, not just the data in the displayed worksheet.

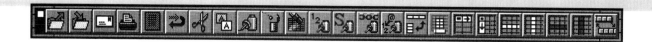

Using 3D Ranges

3D ranges are labeled using the first and the last cell in the range, just as in a one-dimensional range. A 3D range labeled C:A4..F:B6 includes A4..B6 on worksheets C, D, E, and F.

To select a 3D range:

1. Select the range in the first worksheet.

2. Hold down the Shift key while you click on the tab of the last worksheet to be included in the range.

Working with a Collection of Ranges

A collection is more than one range on a single or multiple worksheets in a file. Collections are labeled by indicating each range separated by commas or semicolons. For example, A:A4..A:C6,B:C12..B:G15,D:A2..D:B10 is the label for a collection that includes A4..C6 in worksheet A, C12..G15 in worksheet B, and A2..B10 in worksheet D.

To select a collection:

1. Select the first range in the first worksheet.

2. Hold down the Ctrl key while you select another range in the same worksheet.

3. If necessary, hold down the Ctrl key while you click on the tab of another worksheet in the file.

4. Repeat steps 2 and 3 as necessary.

Selecting a Range of Worksheets

You can also work with a *range* of worksheets (a group of adjacent worksheets in a file). When a range of worksheets is selected, every cell in each worksheet in the range is selected. For example, if you select the range of worksheets beginning with A and ending with C, every cell in worksheets A, B, and C is selected.

To select a range of worksheets:

1. Click on the letter of the first worksheet in the range.

2. Hold down the Shift key while you click on the tab of the last worksheet in the range.

Selecting a Collection of Worksheets

A collection of worksheets is more than one worksheet in a file. The worksheets in a collection are not necessarily adjacent.

To select a collection:

1. Click on the letter of the first worksheet.

2. Hold down the Ctrl key while you click on the tab of the next worksheet to make it current.

3. Then hold down the Ctrl key while you click on the letter of the current worksheet to select it.

4. Repeat steps 2 and 3 until each worksheet you want in the collection is selected.

Deleting Worksheets

Use a worksheet's quick menu to delete the worksheet from a file.

- Right-click on the tab of the worksheet you want to delete, and then select Delete in the quick menu that appears.

Delete...

WARNING

If you delete a worksheet, all the data on the worksheet is also deleted. Instead of deleting a worksheet and possibly losing important data, just click on the New Sheet button to add a new worksheet.

- Or, right-click on the worksheet letter of the current worksheet, and then select Delete in the quick menu.
- To delete a selected range of worksheets, choose Edit ➤ Delete (Ctrl+–)

NOTE

You cannot delete a collection of worksheets. Instead, delete each worksheet individually.

Naming a Worksheet

You can assign a meaningful name to each worksheet in a file. For instance, a worksheet that contains the sales data for the first quarter can be named Qtr1. Then, you can make your formulas easier to understand by using the *name* of the worksheet instead of its letter in formulas that reference data on the worksheet.

N O T E

The name assigned to a worksheet appears on the worksheet's tab. 1-2-3 also assigns the worksheet its own letter, the same one that appears just to the left of the column headings.

There are several rules to remember when naming worksheets:

- Worksheet names can contain up to 15 characters consisting of uppercase or lowercase letters, numbers, and the underscore character.

- Do not name a worksheet with an @function name, the name of a key on the keyboard, or a name that looks like a cell address.

- Use a worksheet name only once in a file.

- Do not begin the name of a worksheet with @, $, or !, although you can use those characters later in a name.

- Do not use the following characters in a worksheet name: , (comma), ; (semicolon), . (period), + (plus sign), – (minus sign), * (asterisk), / (slash), & (ampersand), > (greater-than sign), < (less-than sign), # (pound sign), ((open parenthesis),) (close parenthesis), ^ (caret), and = (equals sign).

To name a worksheet:

1. Double-click on the tab of the worksheet to be named. The tab changes into a text box with the insertion point already in it.

2. Type the name for the worksheet.

3. Press ↵ to name the worksheet.

To change the worksheet's name back to its assigned letter, double-click on the tab and press Del or Backspace, and then press ↵.

Managing the Display of Worksheet Tabs

1-2-3 contains several tools to help manage the worksheets in a multiple-worksheet file. You can control how or when worksheet tabs are displayed, and change the color of a selected worksheet tab so it can be easily distinguished among all the worksheets in a file.

Controlling Worksheet Tabs

Use buttons on the worksheet tabs line to control how or when the tabs are displayed.

- Click on the Hide or Show Tabs button to toggle the display of worksheet tabs. When worksheet tabs are hidden, you can see an extra row of data in the worksheet.

- When your file contains many worksheets, there may not be enough room to display all the tabs simultaneously. Click on the → scroll tab button to scroll the display of worksheet tabs to the right or the ← scroll tab button to scroll the tabs displayed to the left.

Changing the Color of a Tab

It may be helpful to change the color of some tabs in your multiple-sheet files. For example, you could assign one color to the tab of each worksheet that contains a chart, and another color to the primary data.

NOTE

You can even color-code the tabs in your multiple-worksheet files so you can see at a glance which worksheet contains a specific type of data. For example, all tabs of worksheets that contain a chart can be red, and all tabs of worksheets that contain your primary data can be blue.

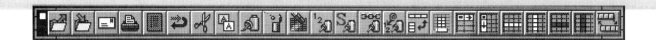

To change the color of a worksheet tab:

1. Right-click on the tab, and then select Worksheet Defaults in the quick menu that appears. The Worksheet Defaults dialog box, shown in Figure 6.4, appears.

Worksheet Defaults...

FIGURE 6.4

Display the Worksheet Defaults dialog box when you want to assign a color to a worksheet tab.

2. In the Colors area of the dialog box, click on the Worksheet tab drop-down list button to display a color palette. The currently selected color appears surounded by a flashing white frame.

3. Click on the color you want in the palette.

4. Click on OK to change the color of the selected tab.

Displaying Several Worksheets Simultanously

To display up to three adjacent worksheets simultaneously in a multiple-worksheet file, switch to Perspective view. Worksheet tabs are hidden when 1-2-3 is in Perspective view.

1. Click on the tab of the first worksheet you want to display.

2. Select View ➤ Split to display the Split dialog box, shown in Figure 6.5.

FIGURE 6.5

Display the Split dialog box when you want to switch to Perspective view to simultaneously display up to three worksheets in the same file.

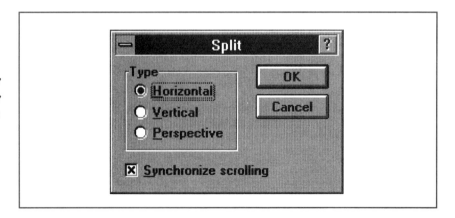

3. In the Type area, click on the Perspective option button.

4. Click on OK.

OK

Click in one of the displayed worksheets to make it the current worksheet. Or, press Ctrl+PgUp to activate and, if necessary, display the next worksheet in the file, or Ctrl+PgDn to activate and, if necessary, display the previous worksheet in the file.

NOTE

Press Home to move to the beginning of the current worksheet. Press Ctrl+Home to move to the beginning of the first worksheet in the file. Choose View ➤ Clear Split to return to the default view.

Grouping Worksheets in a File

To make worksheets in a file appear with exactly the same number formats, fonts, text attributes, colors, alignments, row heights and column widths, frozen titles, and page breaks, change the individual worksheets into a *group*. Each worksheet in the file is included in the group.

WARNING

Every formatting action you perform on the current worksheet also takes place in each worksheet in the file if you have grouped them. For example, if you delete a row of data in one worksheet, the same row is deleted in each worksheet in the file. You may lose valuable data!

To group the worksheets in a file:

1. Right-click on one of the worksheet tabs to display the quick menu, and then select Worksheet Defaults. The Worksheet Defaults dialog box, shown in Figure 6.4, appears.

2. In the Other area, select the Group Mode check box.

3. Click on OK.

> **T I P**
>
> **When you are working in group mode, switch to Perspective view to see how the changes made to the current worksheet affect the other worksheets in the file.**

To end group mode, display the Worksheet Defaults dialog box again, and then clear the Group Mode check box and click on OK. Any formatting changes that were made during your work session in group mode remain in each worksheet.

CHAPTER SEVEN

Creating and Editing
a Chart

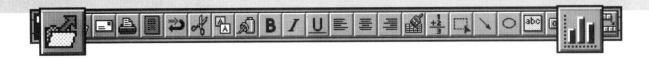

1-2-3 MAKES CREATING a *chart* (a picture of the data) very simple. Create a chart from worksheet data when you want to present trends in or relationships between the data. 1-2-3's charts are *dynamic*—they are automatically updated to reflect changes made to the data on which the chart is based.

A chart can appear on the same worksheet as the data used to compile it, on a separate worksheet in the same file, or in different file altogether. Charts are saved in the same file as the worksheet on which they appear.

Drawing the Chart

Let's use the data on the SALES.WK4 worksheet to add a chart to the file.

1. Display the Default Sheet SmartIcon set to begin this chapter. If necessary, click on the Open button on the Default Sheet SmartIcon set to open the SALES.WK4 file.

2. If you froze titles on the worksheet in Chapter 4, choose View ➤ Clear Titles to remove the frozen titles from the worksheet.

You can tell if there are frozen titles on the worksheet if you cannot select any cell in rows 1 through 4 or in column A.

3. Click on the New Sheet button on the right side of the worksheet tabs line to insert a new worksheet.

4. Click on the Chart button on the Default Sheet SmartIcon set. The Chart Assistant dialog box, similar to that in Figure 7.1, appears.

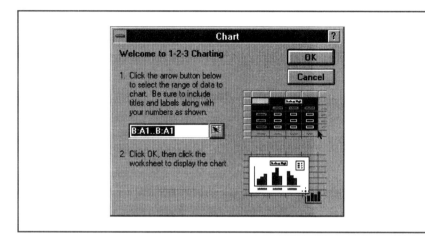

FIGURE 7.1

Click on the Chart SmartIcon to display the Chart dialog box when you want to draw a chart in a worksheet.

5. Click on the selection pointer button beside the text box in the Chart dialog box to change the mouse pointer into a selection pointer.

6. Click on worksheet tab A, and then drag through A4..E7 to select the data for the chart. When you release the mouse button, the Chart dialog box reappears.

7. Click on OK to remove the Chart dialog box and return to worksheet B.

8. Click in the worksheet to have 1-2-3 create the chart in the default chart size.

9. Or, move the mouse pointer into the worksheet, where it changes into a chart drawing tool with a crosshair. Position the crosshair where you want to begin the chart, and then drag the tool down

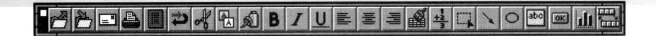

and to the right to create the chart. As you drag, an outline of a rectangle appears where the chart will be drawn. When you release the mouse button, the chart appears, as shown in Figure 7.2.

N O T E

When you select the data and then click on the Chart button to draw the chart on the same worksheet, the Chart dialog box does not appear. Instead, just click in the worksheet to create the chart.

FIGURE 7.2

Use data entered in the SALES.WK4 worksheet to create a bar chart, 1-2-3's default chart type.

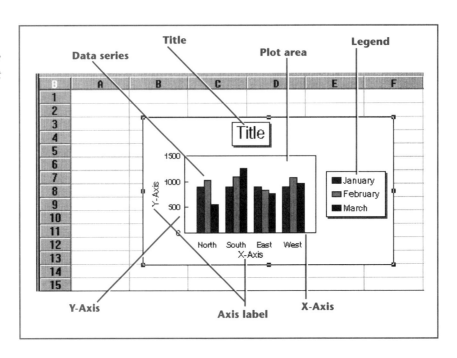

The chart is automatically selected when it appears in the worksheet, and the Default Chart SmartIcon set replaces the previously displayed set. When the entire chart is selected, it appears with eight small black squares, called *handles,* on its borders.

Elements of a Chart

The chart in Figure 7.2 is composed of several different elements, described in the following list:

- The *data series* are the bars that illustrate the values selected to plot the chart. In this example, the data series show the monthly sales data for each region, the values in A:B5..A:E7.

- The chart contains two axes, the horizontal *x-axis* and the vertical *y-axis*. The x-axis plots the data by categories. The y-axis plots the data by values.

- Each axis can have a descriptive name, called the *axis label*.

- The region of the chart that contains both the data series and the axes is called the *plot area*.

- The chart's *title* appears in a text box.

N O T E

If we had entered a description of the contents of the worksheet and selected it along with the data used to plot the chart, it would appear in the title text box on the chart.

- The *legend* describes each data series on the chart. In this example, the legend is the data that was selected in column A.

 Each element of the chart can be selected individually. For example, click on the title of the chart to edit or enhance its appearance. When an element of the chart is selected, it appears surrounded by four handles. The Chart SmartIcons will also appear when any element in the chart is selected.

Changing the Chart Type

By default, 1-2-3 creates a bar chart. However, if a bar chart is not the best choice to illustrate your data, you can change the chart to any of several different chart types and styles.

N O T E

The style of a chart depends on the type of chart displayed. For example, if your chart is a bar chart, you can choose among the standard bar, stacked bar, and comparison stacked bar styles.

1. If necessary, click in the white space near the edge of the outer frame of the chart to select the chart.

 2. Click on the Chart Type button on the Default Chart SmartIcon set to display the Type dialog box, shown in Figure 7.3.

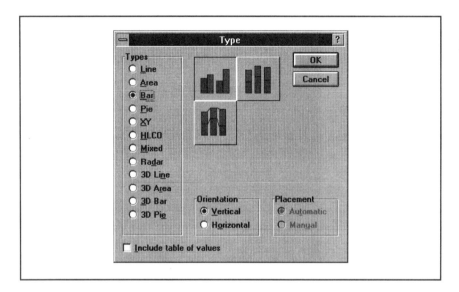

FIGURE 7.3

Display the Type dialog box to choose any of 1-2-3's available chart types and styles.

3. Click on the option button for the type of chart you want in the Types area.

4. Click on the picture that displays the style for the chart.

5. In the Orientation area of the dialog box, select the Vertical option button to place the x-axis at the bottom of the chart, or the Horizontal option button to place the y-axis at the bottom of the chart.

6. Click on OK to change the type of chart.

```
OK
```

Some of the most common chart types and styles appear as icons on the Default Chart SmartIcon set. Select the chart, and then click on one of the following SmartIcons on the Default Chart SmartIcon set to change its type and style.

 A *vertical bar* chart (the default chart type) illustrates the relationship of individual values. The x-axis is at the bottom of the chart, and the data series are plotted vertically along the y-axis.

 A *3D vertical bar* chart displays the data series, categories, and values as three-dimensional.

 A *vertical line* chart displays each value selected as a *data point* (a value in a data series) connected with a line. Use line charts to display and compare actual values.

 A *vertical area* chart is a stacked line chart, with each data series appearing above the previous one. Use area charts to illustrate trends in your data.

 A *pie* chart compares each data series (a slice of the pie) as a percentage of the total value of the data ranges in the chart.

 A *3D pie* chart illustrates three-dimensional pieces of a pie chart comparing each data point to all the data plotted.

Formatting the Chart

Each element of the chart can be changed so the chart will better illustrate the point you want to make with your data. You can also enhance the chart by moving some elements. Begin by selecting the element you want to format.

NOTE

The mouse pointer changes to indicate what type of element you are selecting. For example, as you point to the text in the title text box, the mouse pointer appears with an "A" attached to indicate the element is text.

Adding a Descriptive Title to the Chart

Let's replace the chart's current title with a descriptive title.

1. Right-click on the title text, and then select Headings in the quick menu to display the Headings dialog box, shown in Figure 7.4.

2. Type **Regional Sales Data** in the Line 1 text box in the Title area.

Clear
Headings...
Font & Attributes...

FIGURE 7.4

Display the Headings dialog box to change the chart's title and subtitle or add notes to the chart.

Headings [?]

Title
Line 1: [Title]   ☐ Cell   [OK]
Line 2: [   ]   ☐ Cell   [Cancel]
Placement: ○ Left ⦿ Center ○ Right ○ Manual

Note
Line 1: [   ]   ☐ Cell
Line 2: [   ]   ☐ Cell
Placement: ⦿ Left ○ Center ○ Right ○ Manual

3. Click in the Line 2 text box, and then type **First Quarter 1995**.

4. Click in the Line 1 text box in the Note area, and then type **January sales were flat**.

5. Click in the Line 2 text box in the Note area, and then type **March sales were erratic**.

6. Click on OK.

The chart now appears with a descriptive title, a subtitle, and two footnotes at the bottom of the chart. Each of these is an individual chart element.

Changing the Axis Titles

Use a similar procedure to edit the titles for both the x- and y-axes.

To edit the x-axis title:

1. Right-click on the current x-axis title, and then select X-Axis in the quick menu that appears. The X-Axis dialog box, shown in Figure 7.5, appears.

2. Type **National Regions** in the Axis Title text box.

3. Click on OK to change the x-axis title.

To change the title on the y-axis:

1. Right-click on the current y-axis title, and then select Y-Axis in the quick menu that appears. The Y-Axis dialog box, which is similar to the X-Axis dialog box in Figure 7.5, appears.

2. Type **Monthly Revenue** in the Axis Title text box.

3. Click on OK.

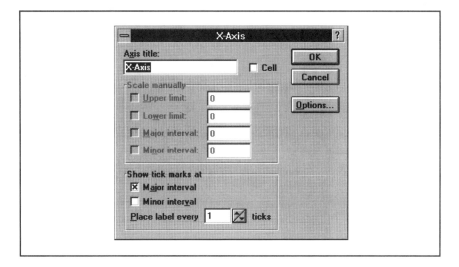

FIGURE 7.5

Display the X-Axis dialog box when you wish to change how the axis is displayed on the chart.

Adding a Grid

To further enhance the chart and make it easier to understand, add a grid to the plot area.

1. Right-click in the white space near the edge of the plot area to display its quick menu.

2. Select Grids in the quick menu that appears. The Grids dialog box, shown in Figure 7.6, appears.

3. Click on the X-axis drop-down button to display the list of grid options.

4. Select Both in the list to display the major and minor grid lines along the x-axis.

5. Click on the Y-axis drop-down button to display the grid line options for the y-axis, and then select Both in the list.

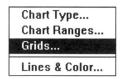

FIGURE 7.6

Display the Grids dialog box when you want to add a grid to a chart.

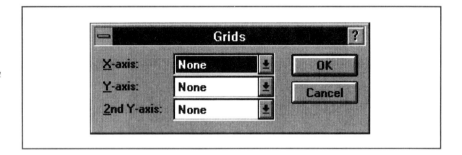

6. Click on OK to display the grid lines in the chart.

Enhancing Chart Text

The text in the chart appears with the font, sizes, and attributes assigned to it by 1-2-3. You can change the format of any of the chart text.

TIP

To change the font or size of any of the chart's text, select the text, and then click on the Font or Point Size button on the status bar to display the corresponding pop-up list. Click on the name of the font or the point size for the selection.

Arial MT

9

1. Right-click on one of the chart's text elements. For example, right-click on the x-axis label.

2. Select Font & Attributes in the quick menu that appears to display the Font & Attributes dialog box, shown in Figure 7.7.

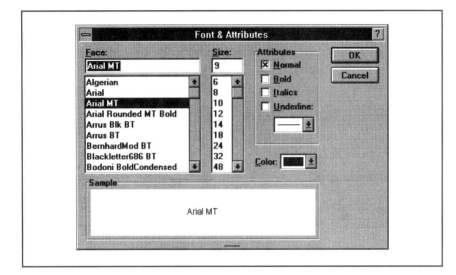

Arial MT

FIGURE 7.7

You must display the Font & Attributes dialog box to change the attributes of one of the chart's text elements.

3. If necessary, scroll through the Face list box to find the name of the typeface for the text, and then select the name.

4. If necessary, scroll through the Size list box, and then select the size for the text.

5. In the Attributes area, select the check box(es) of any of the attributes for the text. For example, select Italics to change the x-axis label.

6. Click on OK to apply the changes to the selected chart element.

OK

> ### NOTE
>
> You can also change the color of selected chart text in the Font & Attributes dialog box. However, you must have a color printer for the text to print in color.

Changing the Number Format of Chart Values

Use the Number Format and Decimal Places buttons on the status bar to format values in a chart.

1. Click on the y-axis values to select them. Each value appears with its own set of handles.

General

2. Click on the Number Format button to display the pop-up list of number formats, and then select US Dollar in the list.

2

3. Click on the Decimal Places button, and then select 0 in the pop-up list.

The y-axis values now appear with dollar signs to indicate that the values represent currency.

Moving and Sizing Chart Elements

Each chart element that appears in a *frame* (a box that surrounds the element) can be moved or sized. For example, the chart's title and subtitle

appear in a single frame, so if you move or size the frame, both elements are moved or sized. You can also move or size the entire chart.

- To move a framed element, move the mouse pointer into the frame until it appears with a white square attached. Then drag the frame to a new position. As you drag, an outline of the frame appears. Release the mouse button when the outline is positioned where you want the frame.

- To move the chart, position the mouse inside the chart until the pointer appears with a black square attached. Then drag the chart to a new position on the worksheet.

- To change the size of a frame or of the entire chart, select the frame or the chart, and then position the mouse pointer over one of its handles until it appears as a four-headed arrow. Drag the handle away from the chart to make it larger, or toward the chart to make it smaller.

Naming the Chart

By default, 1-2-3 assigns a name to each chart in a file. Follow these steps to replace the default name with a descriptive name for the chart.

1. Select the chart, and then choose Chart ➤ Name to display the Name dialog box, similar to the one shown in Figure 7.8.

2. If necessary, highlight the name of the chart to be changed in the Existing Charts list box.

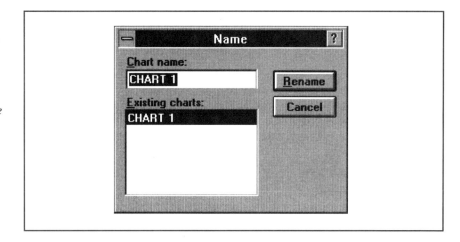

3. Type a new name for the chart in the Chart Name text box. For example, type **First Quarter** as the name for the sample chart.

4. Click on Rename to change the name of the chart.

5. Click on a cell in the worksheet to deselect the chart.

TIP

To quickly move to and select a chart, choose Edit ➤ Go To (F5) to display the Go To dialog box, select Chart in the Type Of Item drop-down list, select the name of the chart in the list box, and then click on OK.

CHAPTER EIGHT

Printing a Worksheet

1-2-3 LETS YOU choose whether to print the entire workbook, the active worksheet, or a selection of your data. You can add *headers* (text that repeats at the top of each printed page) and *footers* (text that repeats at the bottom of each printed page), print titles in a worksheet, and change the margins to enhance the appearance of your printed data. Before you print the data, you can see exactly how it will appear on the page.

 When you are ready to print, switch to the Printing SmartIcon set. Click on the SmartIcons button on the status bar and then select Printing to display the Printing SmartIcon set.

Setting Up the Page

Decide how you want the data to appear on each page before you print it. Then, use the buttons on the Printing SmartIcon set or the options available in the Page Setup dialog box to change the way your data is presented on the printed page. Use the data in the SALES.WK4 workbook to practice printing a workbook. (Fill in additional values to complete the monthly sales figures.)

N O T E

The changes you make using buttons on the Printing SmartIcon set or options in the Page Setup dialog box will appear only on the printed page, not on your screen. To see how your changes will appear when you print the worksheet, use Print Preview. (Information about Print Preview appears later in this chapter.)

Inserting a Page Break

By default, 1-2-3 calculates how many entire rows and columns will fit on a page and automatically places page breaks in your data. Page breaks are not automatically placed between worksheets in a multiple-worksheet file. However, you can manually insert page breaks in and between worksheets to define what you want to appear on each printed page.

- To insert a horizontal page break in a worksheet, select a cell in the row below the last row you want to appear on the page, and then click on the Horizontal Page Break button on the Printing SmartIcon set. For example, to place the first quarter sales figures on the first printed page, select B8, and then click on the Horizontal Page Break button. To insert a horizontal page break between the worksheets, select worksheet B, and then select a cell in row 1 and click on the Horizontal Page Break button.

- To insert a vertical page break, select a cell to the right of the last column you want printed on the page, and then click on the Vertical Page Break button. For example, select worksheet A, select a cell in column G, and then click on the Vertical Page Break button to include the data in columns A through F on the page.

When you insert page breaks in a worksheet, a dashed gray line appears, indicating where the page breaks will occur.

Using Print Titles

Print titles are the rows and columns of data you select in a worksheet to print on each page. Print titles for a printed page are very similar to worksheet titles for a worksheet displayed on your screen. Print titles can consist of adjacent rows or columns, or both rows and columns. The portion of the titles that prints corresponds to the portion of the worksheet that is being printed.

To set print titles for a worksheet:

- Select a range of cells in a column or in adjacent columns, and then click on the Column Print Titles button on the Printing SmartIcon set. For example, select A5..A18 as the range, and then click on the Column Print Titles button to display the data in the range on each printed page.

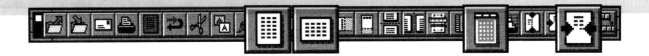

- Select a range of cells in a row or in adjacent rows, and then click on the Row Print Titles button on the Printing SmartIcon set. For example, select B4..F4 in the SALES.WK4 worksheet, and then click the Row Print Titles button to display the data on each printed page.

Changing the Page Orientation

Each page is printed by default in *portrait* page orientation, in which many rows of data will appear on the same page because the page is longer than it is wide. However, if you want to print a worksheet that is composed of many columns you can switch to *landscape* orientation, in which many *columns* of data will appear on the same page because the page is wider than it is long.

To change the page orientation:

- Click on the Landscape Orientation button on the Printing SmartIcon set to change the page orientation to landscape.

- If you want to change the orientation back to portrait (which we don't in this example), click on the Portrait Orientation button on the Printing SmartIcon set.

Changing the Position of the Data

Use any of the following methods to change the position of the data on the printed page:

- To center the data between the left and right margins, click on the Center Horizontally button on the Printing SmartIcon set.

- To center the data between the top and bottom margins, click on the Center Vertically button on the Printing SmartIcon set.

- To center the data on the page both horizontally and vertically, click on the Center All button on the Printing SmartIcon set. For example, activate worksheet A, and then click on the Center All button to center the data on the first two printed pages.

Changing the Size of the Data

Another way to define what will appear on a printed page is to change the size of the data. Data and graphics, such as a chart, can be either reduced or enlarged. However, reduced data can be difficult to read.

Reducing the Data

Use any of the following methods to change the size of the data that will appear on a single page.

- Click on the Size Columns button on the Printing SmartIcon set to reduce the columns so all the columns of data will appear on a single page. If the data consists of many rows, additional pages may be printed in order to print all the rows.

- Click on the Size Rows button to reduce all the rows of data so they appear on a single printed page. If the data consists of many columns, additional pages may be printed to print the data in all the columns.

- Click on the Size Data button to reduce all the data in both rows and columns so it will appear on a single printed page.

Enlarging Data

You can enlarge data that has been reduced to fit on a printed page, or you can enlarge a graphic, such as a chart, to fill an entire page.

To change the size of worksheet data for printing:

1. Click on the Page Layout button on the Printing SmartIcon set to display the Page Setup dialog box, shown in Figure 8.1.

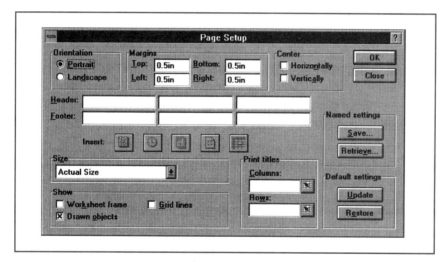

FIGURE 8.1

The Page Setup dialog box contains most of the options necessary to change the way your data appears on a page.

2. To enlarge data that has been reduced for printing, click on the drop-down list button in the Size area of the dialog box, and then select Actual Size in the list.

3. Click on OK.

OK

Changing the Size of a Chart

To either reduce or enlarge the size of a chart on the printed page:

1. Select the chart you created in Chapter 7, and then choose File ➤ Page Setup to display the Page Setup dialog box, similiar to the one shown in Figure 8.1.

2. Click on the drop-down list button in the Size area to display the sizing options for the chart. The options are described below.

> **Actual size** When you select this option, the printed chart, which begins at the top-left edge of the page, is the same size as it is on the screen.

> **Fill page** If you select this option, the chart is enlarged or reduced to fit on the page. However, the proportions of the chart are changed.

> **Fill page but keep proportions** When you select this option, the chart is enlarged or reduced to fit on the page without changing its proportions. Select this option to print the sample chart.

3. Click on OK, and then select a cell in worksheet B.

Adding Headers and Footers

When you place headers and footers on a page in 1-2-3, headers appear below the top margin and footers appear above the bottom margin. A header or a footer can contain up to 512 characters, but any characters beyond the right margin will not print.

There are two rules for displaying special characters in a header or footer:

- Do not use the | (vertical bar character) at all.

- Type an apostrophe before any of these characters to display them in a header or footer: @ (at sign), + (plus sign), # (pound sign), ^ (caret), or \ (backslash).

1. Click on the Page Layout button on the Printing SmartIcon set to display the Page Setup dialog box, similar to the one shown in Figure 8.1.

2. Click in the left Header/Footer text box, and then type the characters you want to align on the left side of the header or footer.

3. Type the characters you want to align in the center of the header or footer in the middle text box. For example, type **Page** and press the spacebar in the Footer text box.

4. Type the characters you want to align on the right of the header or footer in the right text box.

5. Click on any of the following buttons to insert the corresponding information in one of the Header/Footer text boxes at the location of the insertion point.

 Click on the Date button to insert the date set in your computer. The date will be updated each time you print the worksheet.

 Click on the Time button to insert the time set in your computer. The time will be updated each time you print the worksheet.

Click on the Page Number button to insert the page number of the printed page. For example, with the insertion point placed after the space in the middle Footer text box, click on the Page Number button in the Insert area in the Page Setup dialog box.

Click on the File Name button to place the name of the file that contains the data being printed in the header or footer.

Click on the Contents button and then type the cell reference in the text box to place the contents of a cell in a header or footer.

6. Click on OK.

Changing the Margins

By default, the page margins are set at one-half inch because most printers cannot print within one-half inch of the edge of the page. You can increase the page margins, but if you do, fewer rows and columns of

data will appear on each page. The margins are automatically set in inches.

1. Click on the Page Layout button on the Printing SmartIcon set to display the Page Setup dialog box, shown in Figure 8.1.

2. Highlight the characters in the Top, Left, Bottom, or Right text box in the Margins area, and then type **1** to increase the margin to one inch.

3. Repeat step 2 for each margin you want to increase.

4. Click on OK.

Previewing Your Document

Use Print Preview to display each page of the printed worksheet. If the page does not appear exactly as you want it to, change the appropriate setting in the Page Setup dialog box.

1. Select worksheet A, and then select A:B5..A:F18.

NOTE

Remember, earlier you defined print titles for the worksheet. If you do not select the data, the titles will appear twice on each page—once because they are part of the worksheet data, and again because they are print titles.

2. Click on the Print Preview button on the Printing SmartIcon set. The Print Preview dialog box, shown in Figure 8.2, appears, with Selected Range already selected as the Preview option.

FIGURE 8.2

Choose how much of the workbook you want to preview in the Print Preview dialog box.

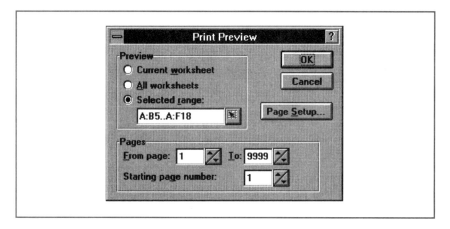

3. Click on OK to display the Print Preview window, similar to that in Figure 8.3.

Click on any of the following SmartIcons to manipulate the pages while the Print Preview window is displayed:

Click on the Next Page button on the Print Preview SmartIcons to display the next printed page.

Click on the Previous Page button to display the previous printed page.

When you click on the Enlarge button, the page is enlarged on the screen.

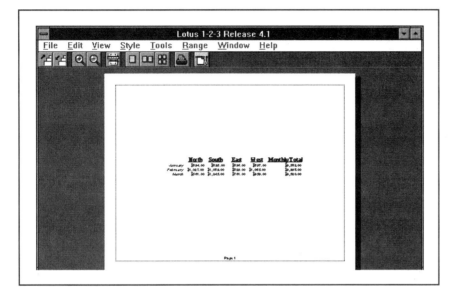

FIGURE 8.3

When you choose Print Preview, the active worksheet appears in the Print Preview window.

Click on the Reduce button to reduce the size of the page on your screen.

Click on the Page Layout button to display the Page Setup dialog box when you need to change any of the page settings.

When you click on the Single Page button one printed page is displayed in the Print Preview window.

Click on the Facing Pages button to preview how facing pages will appear when they are printed.

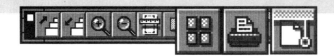

 Click on the Multiple Pages button to display four pages. Click again to display nine pages in the Print Preview window.

 When you are ready to print the worksheet, click on the Print button. The Print dialog box appears. See "Printing the Data" below for additional information.

 Click on the Close button to close the Print Preview window and return to your document.

Printing the Data

Once you have defined how the data will appear on the page and previewed (and approved) the printed document, you are ready to print the data.

N O T E

The printer that is set up to print documents in any other Windows application is the printer 1-2-3 will use to print the data.

 1. Click on the Print button on the Printing SmartIcon set to display the Print dialog box, shown in Figure 8.4.

2. Select one of the options, described below, in the Print area of the dialog box.

> **Current Worksheet** To print data on the active worksheet, select this option.

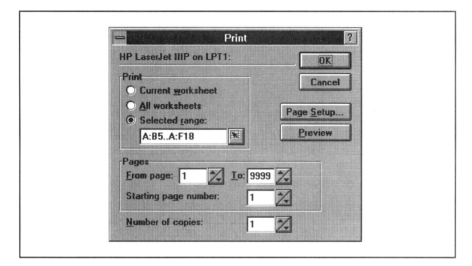

FIGURE 8.4

The Print dialog box appears when you click on the Print button or select File ➤ Print (Ctrl+P).

All Worksheets To print all the data in the workbook including charts, select this option.

Selected Range Select this option to print only selected data, as in this example. If a chart is selected, the option is called Selected Chart.

3. Click on OK to print the selected range.

OK

3

Ami Pro

Creating a
Document

AMI PRO IS a whiz at helping you start almost any type of document, from reports to fax cover sheets. Ami Pro documents are created using *style sheets*—saved collections of *styles* (the formatting and enhancements applied to the text in a paragraph). In Ami Pro, a specific style is applied to each paragraph, so your documents are consistently formatted and professional-looking.

Starting Ami Pro

To start Ami Pro when you are ready to begin creating a document:

1. Click on the Start Lotus Ami Pro button on the SmartCenter SmartIcon set.

2. If Ami Pro appears with the Ami Pro SwitchKit displayed, click on the Exit button below the SwitchKit window to close the SwitchKit. The Ami Pro window, shown in Figure 9.1, appears.

The Ami Pro Window

The Ami Pro window is composed of several parts, which are labeled in Figure 9.1 and described below:

- The SmartCenter SmartIcon set appears on the right side of Ami Pro's title bar. Click on one of the buttons on the SmartCenter SmartIcon set to start or switch to another SmartSuite application.

- The *document window*, between the ruler and the horizontal scroll bar, is where text or graphics are entered in the document. The active document window is the one that contains the *insertion point*, the flashing vertical line that indicates where the next character typed will appear.

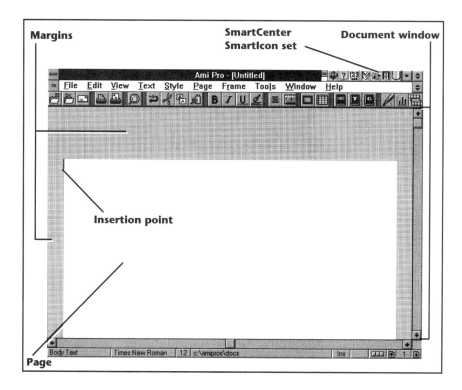

FIGURE 9.1

Each time you start Ami Pro, a new, blank document appears in the Ami Pro window.

- The blue (or gray, on a monochrome monitor) area directly below the ruler is the *margin* of the document. Notice that both the top margin and the left and right margins appear in Figure 9.1. By default, Ami Pro displays each page in *WYSIWYG* (what you see is what you get) viewing mode. (WYSIWYG means that anything you see on the screen will also appear in the printed document.) Because the page margins appear on a page, they also appear in the Ami Pro window.

- The white area within the margins is the *page*, the area of the paper that is within the margins on the printed page.

Entering Text in a Document

To enter text in a document, just begin typing. As you type each character, the insertion point moves toward the right. When the insertion point reaches the edge of the page, the text automatically *wraps* to the next line (begins a new line).

Each time you press ↵, the insertion point also moves to the beginning of the next line. However, although by default you cannot see it in the document, when you press ↵ you also start a new paragraph. To begin a new line of text without starting a new paragraph, hold down the Ctrl key while you press ↵.

> **NOTE**
>
> To display carriage returns (paragraph marks) and tabs in a document, choose View ➤ View Preferences, select the Tabs And Returns check box, and then click on OK.

Entering a Short Line of Text

As an example, let's write a letter. To begin the return address in a business letter (supposing this company doesn't have its own letterhead):

1. Type **Evergreen Nursery and Landscaping, Inc**., and then press Ctrl+↵.

2. Type **1234 Main Street** and press Ctrl+↵.

3. Type **Portland, Oregon 97208**, and then press ↵ to begin a new paragraph.

Entering the Date or Time

Usually the date appears below the return address in a letter. There are two different ways to enter the date set in your computer in an Ami Pro document—enter the current date setting as text, or enter the system date, which will automatically be updated each time you open the document.

NOTE

Of course, you can also type any date or time you want in any style in a document.

1. Press ↵ again to enter a blank line below the return address.

2. Choose Edit ➤ Insert ➤ Date/Time to display the Insert Date/Time dialog box, shown in Figure 9.2.

3. In the Insert area of the dialog box, Today's Date is selected by default. Use it to enter the date set in your computer as text. Or, select the System Date option button to enter your computer's date setting so it automatically updates each time you open the document.

FIGURE 9.2

Use options in the Insert Date/Time dialog box to enter the date or time in a document.

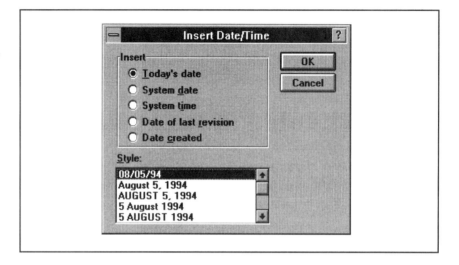

4. In the Style area, highlight the way you want the date to appear in the document. For example, highlight the second style in the list.

5. Click on OK to insert the date.

NOTE

To enter the current time set in your computer, select the System Time option button and click on OK in the Insert Date/Time dialog box. The time is updated whenever you open the document and the page containing the time is displayed.

Entering the Inside Address and the Greeting

Press ↵ twice, and then enter the following text for the letter's inside address and greeting. Remember to press Ctrl+↵ to begin a new line of text without beginning a new paragraph, and ↵ to begin a new paragraph or insert a blank line.

> Mr. Walter Smith
> 8214 Appletree Avenue
> Atlanta, Georgia 30301
>
> Dear Mr. Smith:

Entering Text in the Rest of the Letter

Press ↵ twice, and then enter the following text to complete the body of the letter:

> Thank you for your purchase order, No. 63428, for six weeping willow trees. I am sorry to inform you that they are temporarily out of stock.
>
> I hope this has not caused you any inconvenience. We expect a new shipment within a week of this letter. Your order will be sent as soon as possible after we receive our shipment.

Saving a Document to a File on Your Disk

As you are working in Ami Pro, remember to save early and save often. Saving is especially important if you are working with long documents such as the chapters of a book, reports, or any document you have spent a lot of time creating. When you save a document, it stays on your screen so you can continue to work in it.

To save a document for the first time:

1. Click on the Save button on the Default SmartIcon set to display the Save As dialog box, shown in Figure 9.3.

2. Type a descriptive name of up to eight characters in the File Name text box. For example, type **SMITHLTR**. Ami Pro automatically adds the .SAM file extension.

FIGURE 9.3

The Save As dialog box appears the first time you save a document to a file on your disk.

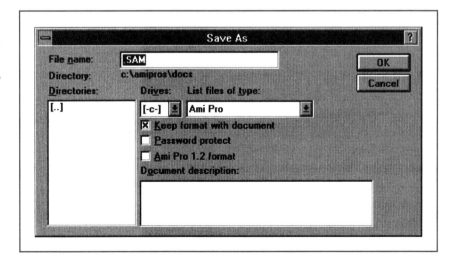

3. In the Document Description text box, type **Letter to Mr. Walter Smith**.

4. Click on OK.

Once you have saved a document to a named file, just click on the Save button to save any changes you make to the document to the same file name. The Save As dialog box will not reappear.

> To save a named file to a different file name, choose File ➤ Save As to display the Save As dialog box. Type a different name in the File Name text box, and then click on OK.

Closing a Document

When you are finished working in a document but want to continue working in Ami Pro, close the document to remove it from your computer's memory.

1. With the document you want to close active on your screen, select File ➤ Close.

2. If you have made any changes to the document since you last saved it, a dialog box similar to that in Figure 9.4 appears.

FIGURE 9.4

If you made any changes to a document since you last saved it, a dialog box appears asking if you want to save the changes.

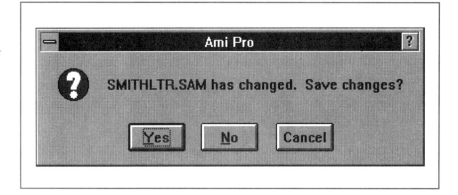

3. Click on one of the buttons described below.

Choose Yes to save any changes made to the document, and then close the file. If you have not previously saved the document to a file name, the Save As dialog box appears. Type a name for the file, and then click on OK.

Choose No button to close the file without saving the changes you made since you last saved the file.

Choose Cancel to return to the active document so you can continue to work in it.

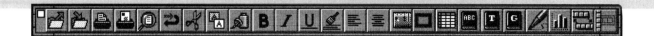

Exiting Ami Pro

When you follow the correct steps to exit Ami Pro, you are prompted to save any documents that you have changed since you last saved them, as well as any unsaved documents.

N O T E

When you are ready to exit Ami Pro, or any computer program, do not turn off the computer until you have exited all the way to the C:\> prompt. For Windows applications in particular, exiting incorrectly can cause some unexpected problems when you next start Windows.

1. Double-click on the Control menu box on the title bar.

2. A dialog box similar to the one shown in Figure 9.4 appears for any open document that you have changed.

3. Click on one of the buttons described below.

Choose Yes to save any changes you made to the active document. If you made any unsaved changes to any *other* open document, the dialog box reappears for that document. If you made changes to a document that you have not saved to a named file, the Save As dialog box appears. Type a name for the file in the File Name text box, and then click on OK.

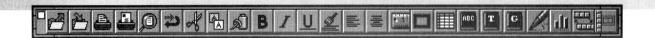

No   Choose No to close the document without saving any changes to it. The dialog box reappears for any other open documents that you have changed.

Cancel   Choose Cancel to keep Ami Pro open and return to the active document.

Editing a
Document

NATURALLY, MOST DOCUMENTS you create will need to be changed in some way. Any changes made to an open document are called *edits* to the document. You will perform some types of editing, such as replacing or deleting text, moving or copying existing text, or entering new text, regularly on most of your documents.

Opening a Previously Saved File

Let's open the SMITHLTR.SAM file we created in Chapter 9.

TIP

By default, the names of the last four files that you opened appear at the bottom of Ami Pro's File drop-down menu. Select File ➤ *Filename* to quickly open one of these files.

---

1. Click on the Start Lotus Ami Pro button on the SmartCenter SmartIcon set to start Ami Pro.

2. Click on the Open button on the Default SmartIcon set to display the Open dialog box, shown in Figure 10.1.

3. Scroll down the Files list box and highlight SMITHLTR.SAM. Notice that the description of the file's contents, which you typed when you saved the file, appears in the Description area of the dialog box.

4. Select the Preview check box to see exactly what the file contains. The file's preview appears in its own window.

Display the Open dialog box when you want to open a file on your hard disk.

5. Click on OK in the Open dialog box. Both the dialog box and the preview window are replaced with the open file.

Opening a New Document

A *style*, as you may remember from Chapter 4, is a set of all the formatting, such as the font, size, and attributes, that is applied to a selection. In Ami Pro, a style also includes the paragraph's line spacing, indentation, and alignment.

A style is applied to each paragraph in an Ami Pro document rather than to only selected text. Ami Pro's paragraph styles are defined, named, and saved in a *style sheet*, a file that contains all the paragraph styles and the document's page layout. Each Ami Pro document is based on the style sheet that is assigned to the file.

N O T E

The new, empty document that appears when you first start Ami Pro is based on the Default style sheet.

In Ami Pro, as many as nine documents can be open simultaneously. Follow these steps to create a new document while the SMITHLTR.SAM file is open.

1. Select File ➤ New to display the New dialog box, shown in Figure 10.2.

FIGURE 10.2

Each time you create a new document, you must select the style sheet on which the document will be based.

New

Each new Ami Pro document has a style sheet associated with it. The style sheet acts as a template for the document.

OK

Cancel

Style sheet for new document:

Article - paragraph styles for professional publications
Basic - Body Text & Body Single paragraph styles
Calendar - daily by half hour, with to do list
Calendar - monthly, automated
Calendar - monthly, from Lotus Organizer
Calendar - weekly by hour, with to do list
Default - most frequently used paragraph styles
Dissertation - paragraph styles for theses and dissertai

☒ **With contents**   ☒ **List by description**
☒ **Run macro**
☐ **Close current file**   ☐ **Preview**

File name: _default.sty

2. Highlight the description that most closely fits the type of document (or the styles you want to use in the document) in the Style Sheet For New Document list box. If necessary, scroll through the list box until you find a description that meets your needs. For example, highlight Fax—Plain, Without Borders.

NOTE

Some of Ami Pro's built-in style sheets are also templates you can use to define the appearance of a document. A template contains text and/or graphics that will appear in a new document that is based on the style sheet when the With Contents check box is selected.

3. Select the Preview check box to see the contents of the selected style sheet or a sample of a document based on the style sheet.

4. Select Default—Most Frequently Used Paragraph Styles in the list box.

5. Click on OK in the New dialog box.

To activate the SMITHLTR.SAM file (which is still open although you can no longer see it on your screen), select Window ➤ SMITHLTR.SAM.

Making Changes to the Text

As you create documents, you will often wish to change the wording in a paragraph, add more text to the document, or delete text you have already entered. Ami Pro makes it easy for you to edit all your documents with the buttons on the Editing SmartIcon set and the status bar.

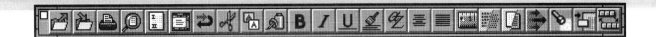

Selecting Text

Before you can replace, move, copy, or perform any other command or
action to text in a document, you must first select the text. The easiest
way to select text is with your mouse. When text is selected, it appears
highlighted on your screen.

Use any of the following methods to select text:

- Drag through the characters you want to select.

- Double-click on a word to select it.

- Hold down the Ctrl key and click in a sentence to select the
  whole sentence.

- To select an entire paragraph, hold down the Ctrl key while you
  double-click in the paragraph.

To deselect a selection, click anywhere in the document.

Changing the Typing Mode

By default, Ami Pro is in *insert typing mode*. Any characters you type are
inserted in the document in the position of the insertion point. If the
insertion point is placed within existing document text, characters that

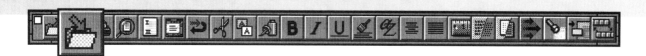

are already to the right of the insertion point move further to the right to make room for the inserted characters.

For example, click after the word "six" in the letter's first sentence. Then press the spacebar and type **beautiful** to insert a space and some text within the sentence.

You can change the typing mode to *typeover*, so the characters you type replace existing document text. To change to typeover mode, click on the Typing Mode button on the status bar. The button displays "Type" to indicate that you are in typeover mode.

Switch to typeover mode, and then click just before the word "willow." Now type **cherry** to type over (replace) the characters.

N O T E

To return to insert typing mode, which most people prefer to use when editing a document, click on the Typing Mode button twice. When you are again in insert mode, "Ins" appears on the button.

Go ahead and save the changes you made to the letter to Mr. Smith.

Moving and Copying Text

There are several ways to quickly move or copy text in Ami Pro. Use either cut, copy, and paste or drag and drop to move or copy selected text to a different location with your mouse. You can also exchange the positions of two adjacent paragraphs using keyboard shortcuts.

Using Cut, Copy, and Paste

Use Cut or Copy to move or copy selected text into the Windows Clipboard. Then, use Paste to copy the contents of the Clipboard to a different location in the same document or to a location in another open document.

1. In the SMITHLTR.SAM document, select the first sentence in the second paragraph of the body of the letter, and then click on the Cut button on the Editing SmartIcon set. The sentence is removed from the document.

2. Select Window ➤ Untitled to display the new document you opened earlier.

3. Click on the Paste button on the Editing SmartIcon set to copy the Clipboard's contents at the beginning of the document.

4. Click on the Paste button again to place another copy of the contents of the Clipboard in the untitled document.

5. Select Window ➤ SMITHLTR.SAM to activate the letter.

6. Select the first paragraph in the body of the letter, and then click the Copy button on the Editing SmartIcon set. The paragraph stays in the letter, and a copy is placed in the Clipboard.

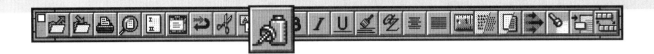

N O T E

Whenever you cut or copy another selection, it replaces the previous contents of the Clipboard. You can paste the current contents of the Clipboard as many times, in as many locations, as
you want.

---

7. Select Window ➤ Untitled and press ⏎ to begin a new
paragraph.

8. Click on the Paste button to copy the new Clipboard contents
in the untitled document.

N O T E

Activate the SMITHLTR.SAM file, and then close it without saving the changes you made when you moved the sentence to
the Untitled document.

Using Drag and Drop

Use drag and drop to quickly move or copy data within a document.
With drag and drop you bypass the Windows Clipboard, so you cannot
paste the selection in more than one location or in a different
document.

- To move text, select the text, and then move the mouse pointer
  over the selection and hold down the left mouse button. The
  mouse pointer appears as an arrow pointing to a vertical bar

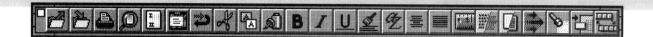

with a pair of scissors attached Drag the mouse pointer until the vertical bar is where you want to place the text, and then release the mouse button to "drop" the selection.

- To copy text, select the text, move the mouse pointer over the selection, and then hold down the Ctrl key while you drag it to another location.

Moving an Entire Paragraph

Use the keyboard to quickly exchange the positions of two adjacent paragraphs. Place the insertion point in one of the adjacent paragraphs, and then:

- Press Alt+↑ to exchange the paragraph that contains the insertion point with the one above it.

- Press Alt+↓ to exchange the paragraph containing the insertion point with the one below it.

Deleting Text

There are several ways to delete text in a document. The one you use will depend on how much text you want to delete at one time.

- To delete the character to the right of the insertion point, press Del.

- To delete the character to the left of the insertion point, press Backspace.

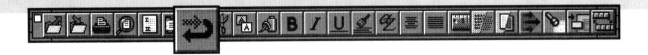

- To delete only selected text, press Del.

- To delete selected text and one character to the left, press Backspace.

- To simultaneously delete selected text and replace it with other text, just type the new text.

Reversing Your Last Command or Action

If you accidentally perform an edit to text in a document, use Undo immediately to reverse the last command or action. To demonstrate Undo, use the Untitled document that is active on your screen.

1. Select the first sentence in the first paragraph, and then press Del.

2. Click on the Undo button on the Editing SmartIcon set immediately to return the deleted text to the document.

> ### N O T E
>
> To undo all the changes made to a document, choose File ➤ Revert To Saved. The document will be returned to the way it appeared when you last saved it.

Moving around Your Document

It is easy to move through a long document using a mouse and buttons that appear on your screen. You've already seen (in Chapter 1) how to use the horizontal and vertical scroll bars to display a different portion

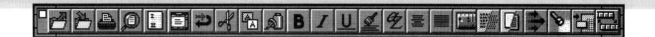

of a document. In fact, there are several ways to move around Ami Pro documents using buttons on the status bar.

Using the Page Arrow Buttons

You can move to a different portion of the active document using Ami Pro's Page Arrow buttons. When you do, the insertion point moves to the page that is displayed.

- Click on the ↑ button on the status bar to move to the previous page in a document.

- Click on the ↓ button on the status bar to move to the next page in a document.

Using Go To

With options in Ami Pro's Go To dialog box, you can move to a specific page in an Ami Pro document. When you use Go To, the insertion point also moves to the specified document location.

1. Click on the Page Status button on the status bar to display the Go To dialog box, shown in Figure 10.3.

2. Select one of the page options in the Go To area of the dialog box. The options are described below.

> **Page number** Click on this option button, and then click on the appropriate button on either side of the text box until the number of the page you want to display on your screen appears.

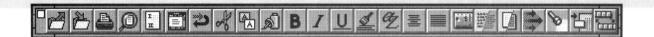

FIGURE 10.3

*To quickly display the
Go To dialog box, just
click on the Page Status
button.*

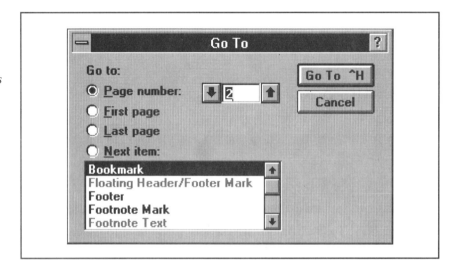

First page Click on this option button to display the
first page in a document.

Last page When you select this option, the last page of
the document is displayed.

3. Click on Go To ^H to display the selected page.

Formatting Document Text

BEFORE YOU HAVE finished working on a document, you may want to change the appearance of some of the document's text. You can change the format of selected text, change the format of an entire paragraph, or apply a different style to a paragraph.

N O T E

Use buttons on the Editing SmartIcon set and the status bar to format selected text in a document. Click on the SmartIcons button on the status bar and then select Editing to display the Editing SmartIcon set.

Formatting and Enhancing Selected Text

Whenever you change the appearance of selected text in a document, you are applying a *format* to the text. Text formatting includes changing the font and size of text or applying an attribute such as boldface or italics.

Usually when you change the format of selected text you want to enhance its appearance for some special reason. For example, you may want the title of a report to appear in a different font, a larger size, and with bold format applied to it to differentiate it from the regular text. Use the SMITHLTR.SAM document you created in Chapter 9 to practice changing the format of selected text.

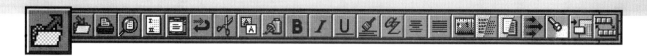

Changing the Font and Size of Selected Text

All text appears in a font, or typeface, that defines how the text appears. By default, the text you entered in the sample letter appears in 12-point Times New Roman font. Use buttons on the status bar to change the font and size of selected text.

> ### NOTE
>
> **The point size is the height of the text. One point equals $1/72$ of an inch.**

1. If necessary, click on the Open button on the Editing SmartIcon set to open the SMITHLTR.SAM document.

2. Select the return address.

3. Click on the Face button on the status bar to display a pop-up list of available typefaces. The fonts that appear in the list are those that your printer can handle.

| Times New Roman |

4. Scroll up through the list, and then select Arial MT to change the font of the selection.

5. Click on the Point Size button on the status bar to display the pop-up list of available point sizes for the Arial MT font, and then select 18 in the list.

| 12 |

Applying Text Attributes

An attribute is a characteristic that can appear along with the typeface of text. Attributes include boldface, italics, and underlining. You can apply as many attributes as you wish to the same selected text. There are buttons on the Editing SmartIcon set that make it very easy to apply attributes to selected text.

1. Select the company name in the return address.

2. Click on the Bold button on the Editing SmartIcon set to apply bold format to the company name.

3. Now select the entire return address and click on the Italics button.

4. Select "as soon as possible" in the second paragraph of the body of the letter, and then click on the Underline button to underline the entire phrase.

To remove an attribute, select the text to which the attribute has been applied and click on the attribute's button. For example, to remove italics from the company name, select only the company name and click on the Italics button.

NOTE

To remove all the formats applied to a selection or to the current paragraph, choose Text ➤ Normal (Ctrl+N). The text is returned to the format specified in the style that is applied to the paragraph. Additional information about paragraph styles appears later in this chapter.

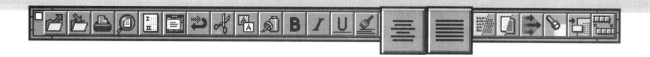

Formatting a Paragraph

Some formats you apply, such as line spacing, indentation, and alignment, affect the entire paragraph. When any of these elements is changed, the change affects the whole paragraph, not just selected text in a paragraph. In fact, it's not necessary to select text to change the format of a paragraph. Instead, just place the insertion point anywhere in the paragraph and apply the new format.

Changing the Alignment

All the paragraphs in the sample letter appear *left-aligned*—they are aligned along the left margin of the page. You can use the alignment buttons on either the Editing or Default SmartIcon sets to easily change the alignment of the paragraph that contains the insertion point.

1. With the company name still selected, click on the Center button on the Editing SmartIcon set. Notice that the entire paragraph is centered between both the left and the right margins.

2. Click in the second paragraph of the body of the letter. Then click on the Justify button to align the paragraph along both the left and the right margins.

N O T E

Notice that the short line of text at the end of the second paragraph is not aligned along both the left and right margins when you click on the Justify button.

3. Select Text ➤ Alignment ➤ Left (Ctrl+L) to return the paragraph to its original left alignment.

N O T E

You can also *right-align* (align the text along the right margin of the page) the paragraph that contains the insertion point by choosing Text ➤ Alignment ➤ Right (Ctrl+R).

Indenting a Paragraph

Notice that none of the paragraphs in the sample letter are indented. Use the ruler to indent the current paragraph. If the ruler does not appear on your screen, click on the Show Ruler button on the Editing SmartIcon set to display it.

1. Place the insertion point in the paragraph whose indentation you want to change. For example, click anywhere in the first paragraph of the body of the letter. Then click anywhere on the ruler to activate it. The active ruler is shown in Figure 11.1.

2. To indent the first line of the paragraph by one-half inch, drag the *Indent First* marker until it is aligned on the one-half inch indicator on the ruler.

3. Repeat steps 1 and 2 to indent the second paragraph.

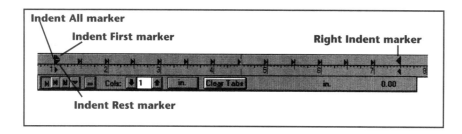

Indent All marker

Indent First marker

Right Indent marker

Indent Rest marker

FIGURE 11.1

Drag the indentation markers on the active ruler to change the indentation of the current paragraph.

There are several other ways you can indent the current paragraph using the indentation markers shown in Figure 11.1. They are described below:

- Drag the *Indent All* marker to indent each line of the paragraph from the left margin.

- Drag the *Indent Rest* marker to indent each line of the paragraph except the first line.

- Drag the *Right Indent* marker to indent each line of the paragraph from the right margin.

To return the current paragraph to the indentation specified in the style applied to the paragraph, choose Text ➤ Indention, select the Revert To Style check box, and then click on OK.

Changing the Line Spacing

Each paragraph in the sample letter is single spaced—no white space appears between the bottom of one line of text and the bottom of the

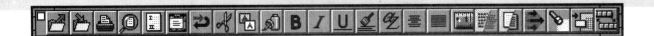

next line. Choose options in the Spacing dialog box to define the spacing between each line of text.

1. Click anywhere in the first paragraph, and then choose Text ➤ Spacing. The Spacing dialog box, shown in Figure 11.2, appears.

2. Click on the Double option button to change the paragraph to double-spaced lines.

3. Click on OK.

4. Repeat steps 1 through 3 to change the line spacing in the second paragraph.

Each time you begin a new paragraph, it appears with the same formats as those applied to the paragraph that precedes it. For example, if you add another paragraph at the end of the letter, it will contain the same formats as those in the second paragraph. The new paragraph in this example will be left aligned and double-spaced, with the first line indented one-half inch.

FIGURE 11.2

Select one of the option buttons in the Spacing dialog box to define how much white space appears between the lines of text in the current paragraph.

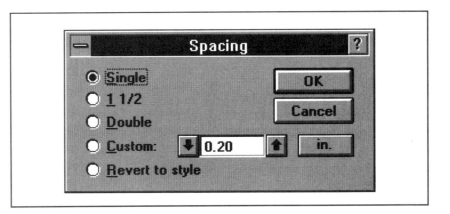

Using Paragraph Styles

Each paragraph in an Ami Pro document is assigned a style. The style assigned to the paragraph determines how the paragraph will appear before you apply any different formats to the paragraph or to selected text.

In the sample letter, each paragraph is assigned the Body Text style, the default paragraph style in the Default style sheet. The Body Text paragraph style automatically left-aligns the text with no indentation, assigns the Times New Roman font in 12-point size (with no attributes), and single-spaces the paragraph. You can use any of the paragraph styles available in the selected style sheet (as you remember, the style sheet is selected when you open a new document), or you can create your own styles.

Creating a Paragraph Style

If you find that you often use the same characteristics for paragraphs in your documents, you can create a style that is based on formatting changes you have applied to a paragraph.

1. Select the first paragraph in the body of the letter.

2. Choose Style ➤ Create Style to display the Create Style dialog box, shown in Figure 11.3.

3. Type a definitive name for the style in the New Style text box. A style name can contain as many as 13 characters, and can include spaces. For example, type **Letter Body** to name a new style.

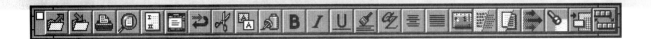

FIGURE 11.3

Display the Create Style dialog box to create a new style for your documents.

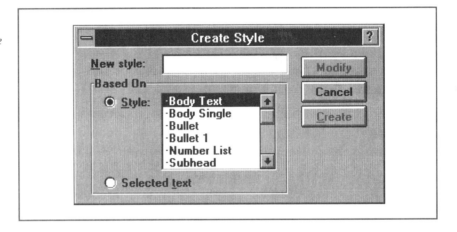

4. In the Based On area of the dialog box, select the Selected Text option button.

5. Click on Modify to define the new Letter Body style. The Modify Style dialog box, shown in Figure 11.4, appears.

6. Click on OK to create the new style.

Assigning a Paragraph Style

Once you have created a style, you must apply it to the paragraph whose style you want to change. For example, although you created the Letter Body style using the formatting applied to the first paragraph, the Body Text style is still applied to it. Use the Style Status button to see the name of the style that is currently applied and to apply a different style to a paragraph.

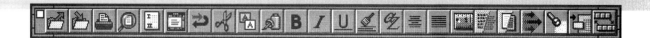

FIGURE 11.4

The Modify Style dialog box contains options for all the formatting that can be saved in a paragraph style.

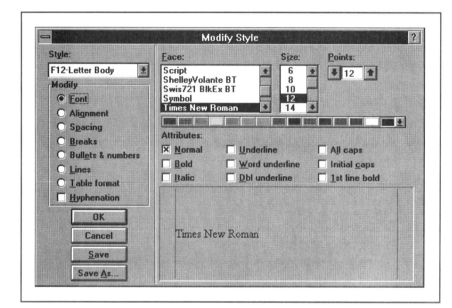

N O T E

The Default style sheet also contains several other paragraph styles. Any of the styles that appear in the pop-up list when you click on the Style Status button can be applied to a paragraph in the document.

---

1. If necessary, click anywhere in the first paragraph to make it current.

2. Click on the Style Status button on the status bar to display a pop-up list of the styles available in the sample letter.

Body Text

3. Select Letter Body in the list to apply that style to the first paragraph.

Using Fast Format

Toggle Ami Pro's Fast Format feature to copy the format of selected text or the style of the current paragraph to other text in the same document.

Copying the Format of Selected Text

If your document contains text that is formatted with the same characteristics you want to apply to other text, use Fast Format to copy the format instead of reapplying the same format to different text.

1. Select the text that contains the format(s) you want to copy, and then click on the Fast Format button on the Editing Smart-Icon set.

2. Move the insertion point to the text you want to format, and then drag to select the text. Release the mouse button to copy the selected format(s) to the text.

3. If necessary, repeat step 2 for any other text in the document.

4. Toggle the Fast Format button off.

Copying the Style of a Paragraph

Use Fast Format to quickly copy the style of the current paragraph to a different paragraph.

1. Click in the paragraph whose style you want to copy, and then click on the Fast Format button on the Default SmartIcon Set. The Fast Format dialog box, shown in Figure 11.5, appears.

2. The Only Paragraph Style option button is already selected. Click on OK to copy the paragraph style.

3. Move the mouse pointer to the paragraph to which you want to copy the selected style, and then select a word in the paragraph.

4. Repeat step 3 for each paragraph to which you want to copy the style.

5. Toggle the Fast Format button off.

FIGURE 11.5

If you do not select text before you click on the Fast Format button on the Default SmartIcon Set, select which formats you want to copy in the Fast Format dialog box.

Fast Format

You do not have any text selected.
What formats do you want to extract?

  ○ Only text font and attributes
  ◉ Only paragraph style

OK
Cancel

Using Style Sheets

A style sheet is a collection of styles that has been saved to a file. Each time a new document is created, you choose which style sheet on which to base the document, and therefore which styles will be available.

> ### NOTE
>
> **A style sheet contains all the information that determines how the document will appear, including the page layout (the margins, paper size, etc.). See Chapter 12 for information about changing the layout of a page.**

However, if you change an existing style or create a new style (as we did in the sample letter), the file that contains the styles is not automatically changed. When you modify an existing style or create a new style to use in a document, the changes you made are saved only in the document and are not available to other documents based on the style sheet. In order to use modified or new styles in other documents, save the style sheet.

Saving a Style Sheet

You can save a style sheet to either the name of the current style sheet's file or to a new style sheet file. Style sheet files are automatically saved to Ami Pro's \STYLES subdirectory.

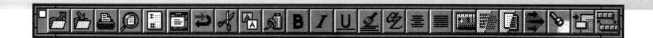

N O T E

When you open a new document, Ami Pro also looks for the available style sheet files in the \STYLES subdirectory.

To save the style sheet with the new Letter Body style, follow these steps:

1. Choose Style ➤ Save As A Style Sheet. The Save As A Style Sheet dialog box, shown in Figure 11.6, appears.

2. Type a name for the new style sheet in the File Name text box. For example, type **MYSTYLES**. Ami Pro automatically adds the .STY extension to the file.

3. Highlight the text in the Description text box, and then type **Default style sheet with Letter Body style added**.

4. If you want to save the text of the letter in the style sheet, select the With Contents check box.

FIGURE 11.6

Display the Save As A Style Sheet dialog box, and then type a name for the new style sheet in the File Name text box.

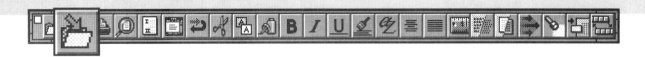

5. Click on OK to save the style sheet.

6. Click on the Save button on the Default SmartIcon set to save the changes to the SMITHLTR.SAM file.

To see the new style file, choose File ➤ New to display the New dialog box, shown in Figure 11.7. The description of the new style file is added, alphabetically at the end of the list of style sheets. Click on Cancel to return to the letter.

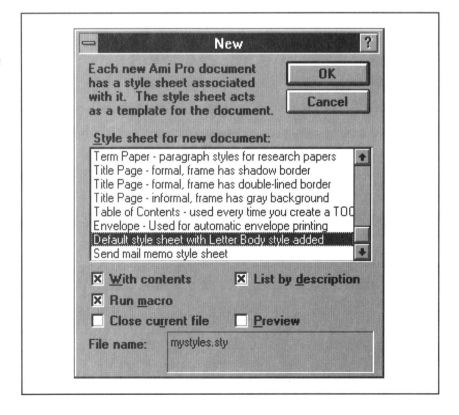

CHAPTER TWELVE

Changing the Format of the Page

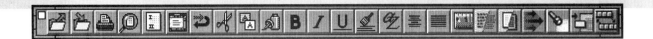

IN AMI PRO, the style sheet on which each document is based also contains information, called the *standard* layout, defining the appearance of each page in the document. This information includes the page margins, the tab stops, whether the document contains headers or footers and page numbers, and whether a border appears around each page. You can change any element of the standard layout when you want to change the appearance of each page in the document.

Begin this chapter by displaying the Editing SmartIcon set.

Using the Ruler to Modify the Page Layout

You can easily change the margins and the number of columns in the current document by using a mouse and the markers and buttons on the active ruler. Click anywhere on the ruler to activate it. The active ruler is shown in Figure 12.1.

Adjusting the Page Margins

To change the margins in the current document, use the margin markers on both the horizontal and vertical rulers. The margin markers on the horizontal ruler are labeled in Figure 12.1

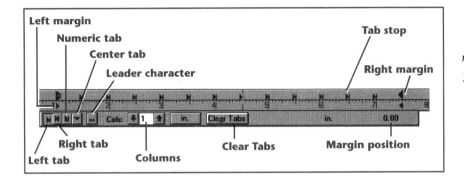

FIGURE 12.1

Click anywhere on the ruler to activate it when you want to change the margins or number of columns in a document, or the tab stops in the current paragraph.

NOTE

To display the vertical ruler, choose View ➤ View Preferences, select the Vertical Ruler check box, and click on OK.

To change the margins in the SMITHLTR.SAM document, make it the active document on your screen.

1. Drag the left-margin marker until it is aligned at the 1-½–inch indicator on the ruler. As you drag, a vertical line appears to show the position of the margin.

2. Drag the right-margin marker until it is aligned at the 7-inch indicator on the ruler.

3. Drag the top-margin marker on the vertical ruler until it is aligned at the 1-½–inch indicator.

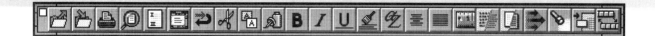

NOTE

To help you correctly position the marker, the current measurement of the selected marker on the horizontal ruler appears on the right side of the active ruler (as shown in Figure 12.1) as you drag.

Notice that the margins that appear on your screen are increased, and the page size is decreased when you follow the steps above. Drag each marker back to its original setting.

Changing the Number of Columns

Use the Columns arrow buttons on the active ruler, shown in Figure 12.1, to change the number of columns in the active document. (Documents based on the Default style sheet automatically contain one column.)

- Click on the ↑ button to increase the number of columns.
- Click on the ↓ button to decrease the number of columns.

Each column has its own margins, which can be changed using the steps outlined previously in "Adjusting the Page Margins."

Setting Tab Stops

Use the tab markers, shown on the active ruler in Figure 12.1, to change the tab stops in the current paragraph. To change the tab stops for all the paragraphs in the document, you must display the Modify Page Layout dialog box.

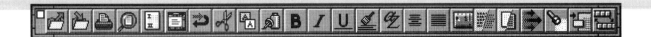

Setting Tab Stops in a Paragraph

If you must change the tab stops in a single paragraph, click anywhere in the paragraph, and then follow these steps:

1. Click in the ruler to activate it.

2. To clear all the tabs, click on the Clear Tabs button on the ruler. Or, to delete one tab stop, just drag it off the ruler.

3. Click on one of the buttons described below to indicate the type of tab you want to set in the paragraph.

- Click on the Left Tab button to create a left-aligned tab stop, in which the characters typed after pressing Tab are aligned at and to the right of the tab.

- Click on the Right Tab button to create a right-aligned tab stop, in which the characters typed after pressing Tab are aligned at and to the left of the tab stop.

- When you click on the Numeric Tab button, you create a numeric tab stop. After you press Tab, the characters are aligned along the numeric character you type (usually a decimal point).

- Click on the Center Tab button to create a center tab stop. The characters you type after pressing Tab are evenly positioned around the tab stop.

- Click on the Leader Character button to add a leader character to the selected type of tab. Each time you click on the button, the leader character changes (and is displayed on the tab stop type buttons), so you can choose the underline character, dashes, periods, or none (the default).

4. Click on the line above the measurement on the ruler to set the type of tab you selected in step 3.

N O T E

When you click on the ruler to position the tab stop, the measurement for the tab stop appears on the right side of the active ruler. If necessary, use the displayed measurement to help you drag the tab stop to an exact position on the ruler.

---

5. Repeat step 4 for each tab you want to set with the same tab type selected.

6. If necessary, select a different type of tab, and then repeat steps 4 and 5.

You cannot drag a tab stop beyond another tab stop that is already set on the ruler or change the type of an existing tab stop. Instead, delete the tab stop you want to move or change by dragging it off the ruler, and then create a new tab stop of the type you want in the correct position.

Setting Tab Stops in a Document

To change the tab stops in each paragraph in the document, change the tab stops in the Modify Page Layout dialog box. The same steps you used to change tabs on the active ruler are also used to change the tabs on the ruler in the Modify Page Layout dialog box. However, any individual paragraphs whose tab stops were previously changed are not changed when you change tab stops in the entire document.

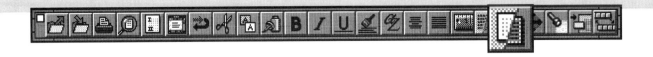

1. Click on the Modify Page Layout button on the Editing SmartIcon set, or move the mouse pointer into the left or right margin and click the right mouse button. The Modify Page Layout dialog box, shown in Figure 12.2, appears.

2. Follow steps 2 through 6 above.

3. Click on OK in the Modify Page Layout dialog box.

Adding a Header or Footer

Placing a *header* (repeating text in the top margin) or a *footer* (repeating text in the bottom margin) is so very simple in Ami Pro that you will

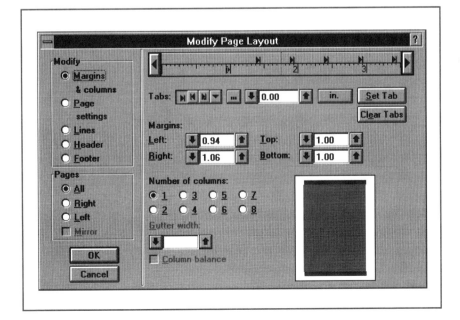

FIGURE 12.2

Display the Modify Page Layout dialog box to change the tab stops in the entire document.

probably want to use headers and footers in virtually all your documents. Use the same editing and formatting methods you use in regular document text to change or enhance the headers and footers.

1. In the SMITHLTR.SAM document, move the mouse pointer into the top margin and then click the left mouse button.

2. Press Ctrl+R to right-align the header.

3. Type **Backorder**.

4. Scroll to the bottom of the page, and then click in the bottom margin.

5. Click on the Center button on the Editing SmartIcon set to center the footer.

6. Type **Page.**

Inserting a Page or Column Break

Ami Pro automatically breaks pages and columns when the text reaches the bottom margin. However, you can define a different location at which to begin a new page or column by inserting a manual page or column break.

> **NOTE**
>
> Display the Long Documents SmartIcon set to use in the rest of this chapter.

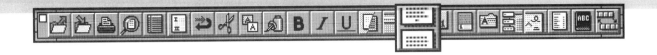

1. With the sample letter active on your screen, click at the end of the first paragraph.

2. Click on the Page Break button on the Long Documents Smart-Icon set to display the Breaks dialog box.

3. Select the Insert Page Break or the Insert Column Break option button to insert a manual page or column break at the location of the insertion point.

4. Click on OK. The text below the first paragraph is moved to the top of the next page.

NOTE

To remove a manual page break or a manual column break, display the Breaks dialog box, choose the Remove Page Break or Remove Column Break option button, and click on OK.

Numbering the Pages

Documents that contain more than one page usually contain page numbers so the reader can keep the printed pages in order. Use Ami Pro's page numbering feature to automatically enter and update the number on each page in a document.

You can insert page numbers anywhere on the page within the margins, or in the top or bottom margin in a header or footer. In the sample letter, the pages will be numbered in the footer. The leading text for the

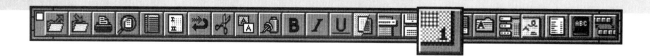

page number is already in the footer of the sample letter. Follow these steps to enter automatic page numbering:

1. Scroll to the footer on either page of the sample letter, and then click just after "Page."

2. Press the spacebar to add a space between the leading text and the number.

3. Click on the Page Number button on the Long Documents SmartIcon set. The Page Numbering dialog box, shown in Figure 12.3, appears.

4. If necessary, click on the Style drop-down list button to display the list of numbering styles, and then click on the style you want for the page numbers.

FIGURE 12.3

Define how the page numbers will appear in the Page Numbering dialog box.

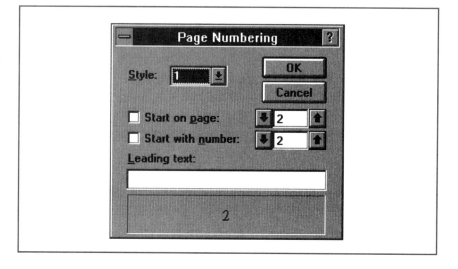

5. Select the Start On Page check box. If necessary, click on the ↑ button to specify a different page on which to begin numbering. For example, click on the ↑ button until 2 appears in the text box to begin page numbering on the second page of the letter.

6. Select the Start With Number check box. If necessary, click on the ↑ button to specify a different number as the first number on the first numbered page. For example, click on the ↑ button until 2 appears in the text box to place the number 2 on the second page of the letter.

7. Click on OK.

Adding a Border to the Page

To enhance a document, add a border around each page. You define exactly where the border is placed in relation to the margins and the edge of the paper.

1. With the sample letter active on your screen, click on the Page Layout button on the Long Document SmartIcon set to display the Modify Page Layout dialog box, shown in Figure 12.2.

2. In the Modify area, click on the Lines option button. The Modify Page Layout dialog box changes to display the line options, as shown in Figure 12.4.

3. In the Around Page area, select the Top and Bottom check boxes to place a border at the top and the bottom of the page.

4. If necessary, select a different style for the line in the Style list box.

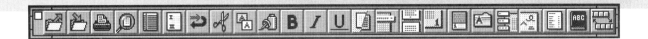

FIGURE 12.4

Define how and where borders appear on each page of a document by selecting Lines in the Modify Page Layout dialog box.

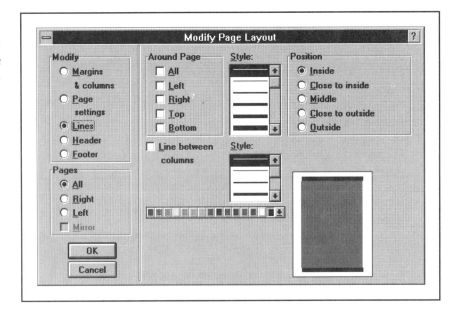

5. In the Position area, select one of the options to define where the lines are placed in relation to the corresponding margin and the edge of the paper. For example, choose Inside to place the line on the top and bottom margins.

6. Click on OK to add the specified border to each page.

CHAPTER THIRTEEN

Using Frames

N AMI PRO, you use frames to place text in the margins or to place graphics anywhere in a document. Creating a frame is like placing a small document within your document—the format of the frame is not affected by any changes you make to the document.

You can use frames as often as you want. Multiple frames can be placed in the same document, or even on the same page.

N O T E

Display the Graphics SmartIcon set to use in this chapter.

Creating a Frame

Place a frame in your document when you want to position text in an unusual location. For example, you can use a frame to create your own letterhead or to place notes in the margins of a document.

N O T E

Any pictures you place in an Ami Pro document are automatically placed in a frame. You can also import a picture into an existing frame. See "Inserting a Picture in a Frame," below.

Open a new document based on the Default style sheet, and then follow these steps to create a letterhead:

1. Click on the Add Frame button on the Graphics SmartIcon set. Move the mouse pointer into the document window, where it changes into a crosshair with a frame attached.

2. Position the crosshair where you want the top-left corner of the frame to appear, and then hold down the left mouse button and drag down and to the right. For example, drag the horizontal scroll box to the left to display the left margin of the page. Place the crosshair in the margin near the top-left corner and hold down the mouse button. Then drag so the frame overlaps the top margin, left margin, and the top of the page. As you drag, an outline of the frame appears.

3. Release the mouse button when the frame is the size and shape you want it to be.

The new frame appears with *handles*, the eight small, black squares that surround the frame, indicating that the frame is selected. To make any changes to a frame, the frame must be selected.

NOTE

To select a frame, click inside it. Click anywhere outside the frame to deselect a selected frame.

Inserting a Picture in a Frame

Often, a letterhead contains a graphic that represents the company's logo or type of business. Ami Pro comes with some built-in clip art files, from which you can choose a picture to place in the frame.

1. Click on the Import Picture button on the Graphics SmartIcon set. A dialog box similar to the one in Figure 13.1 appears.

2. Scroll through the Files list box, and then click on FLOWERS.SDW to place a picture of flowers in the frame.

3. Click on OK to import the picture.

FIGURE 13.1

Select the name of the file you want to place in the frame in the Import Picture dialog box.

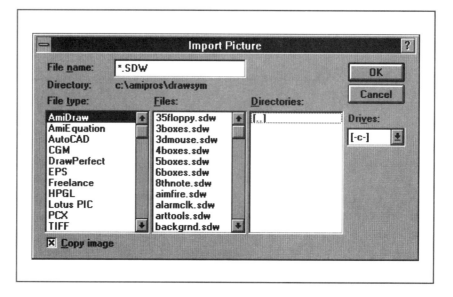

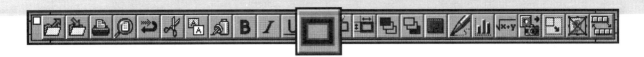

Placing Text in a Frame

To complete the letterhead, create a separate frame for the text, and then type the company's name and address in the frame. In order to enter or edit text in a frame, the insertion point must be in the frame.

1. Click on the Add Frame button, and then draw a frame beside the first frame.

2. Double-click inside the frame to place the insertion point in it. When the insertion point is in the frame, the handles around the frame are gray instead of black.

3. Type **Evergreen Nursery and Landscaping, Inc**. If the frame is not wide enough, the text automatically wraps to the next line.

4. Press Ctrl+⏎ to start a new line of text, and then type **1234 Main Street**.

5. Press Ctrl+⏎ again, and then type **Portland, Oregon 91286**.

Editing Text in a Frame

By default, the Body Text style is applied to text in a frame. However, you can apply a different style to the paragraph, or enhance selected text in a frame.

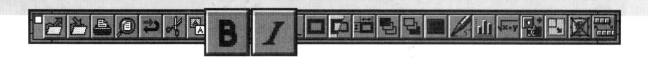

1. Select the first entire line, including any text that wrapped to the next line.

2. Click on the Face button on the status bar, and then select Arial MT in the pop-up list.

3. Click on the Size button on the status bar, and then select 16 in the pop-up list.

4. Select the rest of the text in the frame, and then change it to the 14 point Arial MT font.

5. Click on the Italics button on the Graphics SmartIcon set to italicize the selection.

6. Select all the text in the frame, and then click on the Bold button to apply bold format. Click outside the frame to deselect it.

NOTE

When the horizontal ruler is displayed, the width of a selected frame is reflected on the ruler. When the vertical ruler is displayed, the height of the selected frame appears on the ruler. Use the indentation and margin markers on the rulers to change the margins and indentation of text within the frame.

Editing a Frame

Frames can be moved or sized, copied, deleted, and grouped together. In addition, you can change the borders of a selected frame.

Moving and Copying Frames

Frames (and their contents) can be moved or copied to a location on the same page, to a different page, or even to a different document.

- To move a frame to a different location on the same page, just drag it to a different position. As you drag, the outline of the frame appears. When the outline is in the position where you want it, release the mouse button.

For example, point to the frame that contains the text, and then hold down the left mouse button and drag the frame until it slightly overlaps the frame with the flowers. When you release the mouse button, the frames appear similar to those in Figure 13.2.

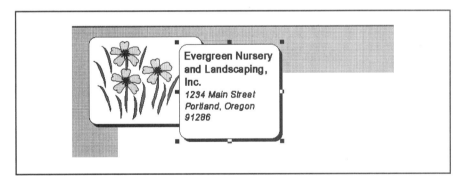

FIGURE 13.2

You can even overlap frames to create a different look.

- To move a frame to a different page or document, select the frame, and then click on the Cut button on the Graphics SmartIcon set. Choose Window ➤ *Document Name* to activate the document, click in the location at which you want to place the frame, and then click on the Paste button.

- To copy a frame to a different position on the same page, on a different page, or in a different document, select the frame and then click on the Copy button. Position the insertion point on the page (if necessary, choose Window ➤ *Document Name* to activate the document), and then click on the Paste button.

N O T E

To delete a frame and its contents, select the frame and press Del.

Changing the Size of a Frame

Use your mouse to change the size of a selected frame.

- Drag one of the corner handles to simultaneously change both the height and the width of the frame. As you drag, an outline appears in the current size of the frame. Release the mouse button when the outline appears in the size you want for the frame.

In the letterhead, for example, drag the handle in the lower-right corner of the text frame up to decrease its height, and to the right to increase its width. When you release the mouse button, the text in the first line of the frame no longer wraps to the second line. (After the size is changed, you may have to move the text frame lower to better position it in relation to the graphics frame.)

- Hold down the Shift key while you drag a corner handle of the frame to change the size of the graphic in it in relation to the changing size of the frame.

- Drag one of the handles in the center of the top or bottom edge of the frame to change only the height of the frame.

- Drag one of the handles in the center of the left or right edge of the frame to change only the width.

Changing the Order of Overlapping Frames

In Figure 13.2, the frames that were used to create the letterhead were *layered* so the text frame appears over the graphics frame. You can place a different frame on the top or bottom layer of a set of layered frames.

- Select the text frame, and then click on the Send To Back button on the Graphics SmartIcon set to place it under the graphics frame.

- Click on the Bring To Front button to return the text frame to its original position.

Grouping Frames

Ami Pro regards grouped frames as a single entity. Grouping is useful when you have placed two or more frames in a position in which you want them to appear always.

For example, the text and graphics frames of the letterhead should be grouped. Or, place the caption for a picture in a frame, and then group the picture and the caption so they stay together while the document is edited.

1. Click on the text frame in the letterhead.

2. Hold down the Shift key, and then click on the frame with the flowers to select it, too. Handles appear around each frame.

3. Toggle the Group button on the Graphics SmartIcon set on to group the two frames.

If you click on a frame that is grouped with other frames, all the frames in the group are selected.

To ungroup a group, select the group, and toggle the Group button off. Each frame in the former group can be selected and edited separately. Go ahead and ungroup the letterhead frames now.

Changing the Frame's Layout

To define how document text appears in relation to a selected frame or how the frame's borders appear, modify the layout of a selected frame. The layout of the frame includes both the type and the appearance of the frame.

Selecting the Type of Frame

By default, Ami Pro's frames have rounded corners, the document text wraps around the frame, and the frame is placed where you positioned it. You can change any of these elements to change the type of the frame.

1. Select the text frame in the letterhead.

2. Click on the Modify Frame Layout button on the Graphics SmartIcon set to display the Modify Frame Layout dialog box, shown in Figure 13.3.

3. In the Display area, click on the Square Corners option button. A sample of the frame appears in the lower-right corner of the dialog box.

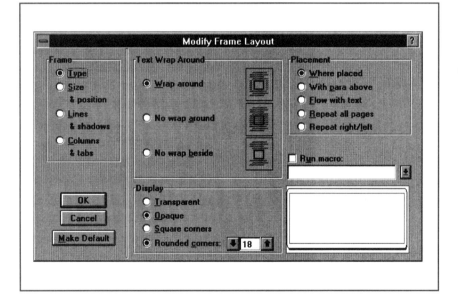

FIGURE 13.3

Display the Modify Frame Layout dialog box to change the type of the selected frame.

Opaque is already selected in the Display area. An opaque frame hides any text or graphics behind it. To display the text or graphics behind the frame, click on the Transparent option button.

4. Click on OK to change the type of the selected frame.

To make the options specified in the Modify Frame Layout dialog box the default options for all future frames in all your documents, click on Make Default before you click on OK.

Changing the Frame's Border

You can also choose which lines, if any, appear around the frame, the style of the lines, and whether a shadow appears around the frame.

1. If necessary, select the text frame.

2. Click on the Modify Frame Layout button on the Graphics Smart-Icon set to display a dialog box similar to that in Figure 13.3.

3. In the Frame area, click on the Lines & Shadows option button. The dialog box changes, as shown in Figure 13.4.

4. In the Lines area, clear the All check box to remove all the lines that appear around the frame.

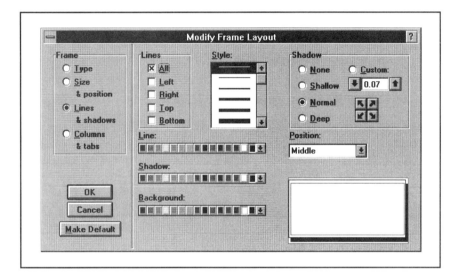

FIGURE 13.4

Choose any of the Lines & Shadows options to change the border around the selected frame.

5. In the Shadow area, click on the None option button to remove the drop-shadow effect from the frame.

6. Click on OK to change the appearance of the frame in the document.

Click anywhere in the document to deselect the frame. The frame is still in the document, even though its borders are no longer displayed.

Notice where the text frame overlaps the graphics frame. Its opaque setting makes it hide the border and drop shadow of the graphics frame.

T I P

To save the letterhead so you can use it for future letters, select Style ➤ Save As A Style Sheet, type a name in the File Name text box, select the With Contents check box, and then click on OK.

Printing Your
Documents

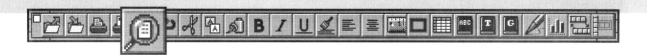

NOW THAT YOU have written and edited the sample letter, you must print it along with an envelope. The printer that is set up to print in Windows is the printer that will print your Ami Pro document.

N O T E
Display Ami Pro's Default SmartIcon set to use in this chapter.

Previewing the Page

Each page of the document appears just as it will when you print it, so you can reduce the size of the page to preview its overall appearance.

- To reduce the size of the current page (change to Full Page view), click on the Toggle Full Page/Layout View button on the Default SmartIcon set.

- Toggle the Toggle Full Page/Layout View button off to return to Layout view (the default).

- To display two pages of the active document, select View ➤ Facing Pages.

- To return to Layout view, click on Cancel in the Facing Pages dialog box when facing pages are displayed.

TIP

Make any necessary changes to the page layout, such as changing the margins or adjusting the width of columns, after you preview it. If you do make changes to the document, preview it again before you print it.

Printing a Document

Now let's print the sample letter.

1. With the sample letter active on your screen, click on the Print button on the Default SmartIcon set. The Print dialog box, shown in Figure 14.1, appears.

FIGURE 14.1

The Print dialog box contains several options you can choose to control the printing operation.

Print	
Number of copies: 1	OK
Page range:	Cancel
○ All	Options...
○ Current page	Setup...
○ From: 1 To: 9999	
including:	
○ Even pages	
○ Odd pages	
○ Both	
Printer: HP LaserJet IIIP on LPT1:	

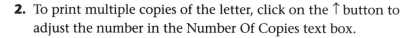

2. To print multiple copies of the letter, click on the ↑ button to adjust the number in the Number Of Copies text box.

3. Click on OK to print the entire letter.

You can also choose exactly which pages you want to print using the options in the Page Range area of the dialog box. Select one of the options described below before you click on OK in the Print dialog box.

- If you select the All option button (which is selected by default), the entire document will print.

- To print the page that contains the insertion point, click on the Current Page option button.

- To print specific pages, click on the From option button, and then click on the ↑ and ↓ buttons in the From and To text boxes to specify which pages you want to print.

Printing an Envelope

Ami Pro is set up to print various sizes of envelopes automatically. If you are using a laser printer that does not have an envelope tray, Ami Pro changes the printer to manual feed mode.

NOTE

Be sure to place the envelope in the printer's tray. Place the envelope face down with the flap opening toward the right to have Ami Pro correctly position the address.

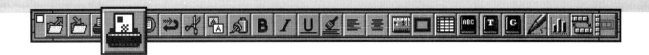

1. Select the recipient's address in the letter.

2. Click on the Print Envelope button on the Default SmartIcon set. The Print Envelope dialog box is displayed.

3. Select the Print Return Address check box. The dialog box changes, as shown in Figure 14.2.

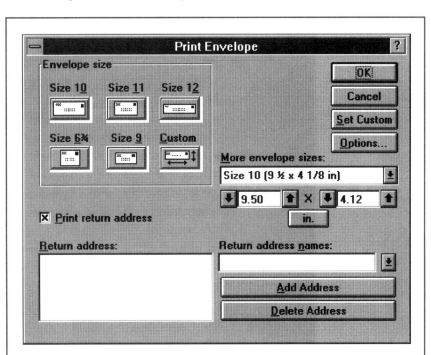

4. In the Return Address text box, type **Evergreen Nursery and Landscaping, Inc.**, and then press ↵ to move the insertion point to the next line.

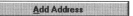

5. Type **1234 Main Street**, and then press ⏎.

6. Type **Portland, Oregon 91286**, and then click on Add Address to add the address to the list of return addresses.

7. Click on OK to print the envelope.

8. If Ami Pro changed your printer to manual feed printing, press the On Line or Form Feed button on the printer to manually send the envelope through the printer.

You can also change the following options in the Print Envelope dialog box:

- To change the size of the envelope, click on one of the sizes in the Envelope Size area of the dialog box.

- To delete one of the return addresses you saved, click on the Return Address Names drop-down button, highlight the name of the person or company you want to delete from the list, and then click on Delete Address. Ami Pro displays a dialog box asking you to confirm that you want to delete the address of the highlighted name—click on Yes.

Printing a Document in Landscape Mode

If you printed the envelope using the steps above, you may have noticed that Ami Pro automatically printed the envelope in landscape mode (the paper is wider than it is high). However, to print any other document in landscape mode, you must adjust several settings.

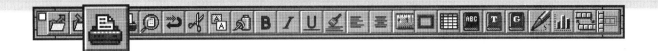

1. Right-click in the left or right margin of the document to display the Modify Page Layout dialog box.

2. In the Modify area of the dialog box, click on the Page Settings option button. The Modify Page Layout dialog box, shown in Figure 14.3 appears.

	Modify Page Layout	?

Modify
- O Margins & columns
- ⊙ Page settings
- O Lines
- O Header
- O Footer

Page Size
- ⊙ Letter   O A4   O A5
- O Legal   O A3   O B5
- O Custom: 8.50 × 11.00   in.

Pages
- ⊙ All
- O Right
- O Left
- ☐ Mirror

Orientation
- ⊙ Portrait
- O Landscape

OK
Cancel

3. Click on Landscape in the Orientation area of the dialog box, and then click on OK.

4. Click on the Print button on the Default SmartIcon set to display the Print dialog box, shown in Figure 14.1. Then click on Setup to display the Setup dialog box for your printer. An example of a Setup dialog box is shown in Figure 14.4.

FIGURE 14.4

If necessary, select the Landscape option in the Orientation area of the Setup dialog box.

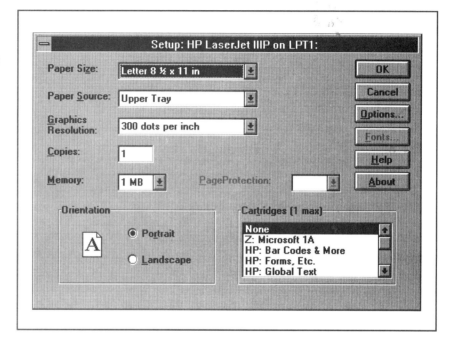

5. Click on OK in the Setup dialog box. Then click on Cancel in the Print dialog box to return to your document.

6. Click on the Toggle Full Page/Layout View button to display the active page, and then click on the ↓ Page Arrow button on the status bar to display each consecutive page of the document. If necessary, repeat steps 1 through 3 for each page of the document.

7. Click on the Print button to display the Print dialog box, and then click on OK to print the document in landscape mode.

NOTE

If the font and size of the characters cannot be printed in landscape mode, you must also change the font to one that appears in the list of available fonts. The easiest way to do this is to display the Modify Style dialog box, change the font in the paragraph style, and then apply the paragraph style to each paragraph you want to print in landscape mode.

PART FOUR

Approach

CHAPTER FIFTEEN

Creating a Database

USE APPROACH TO quickly create a database file for your data. With Approach, you'll never be intimidated by a database again.

Approach comes with a selection of database *templates*, files that contain the structure of a database. To create a database, just choose the template that comes the closest to meeting your needs. For example, you could use the Employees template to create a database for project volunteers or a list of church members.

> ### N O T E
> The Default Browse SmartIcon set is displayed when you first start Approach.

Starting Approach

To create a database, you must first start Approach.

1. Click on the Start Lotus Approach button on the SmartCenter SmatIcon set. The Welcome To Lotus Approach dialog box, shown in Figure 15.1, appears.

2. Click on the Create A New File option button, and then select the name of the type of database you want to create in the list box. For example, to start a new database, highlight Blank Database.

3. Select the Don't Show This Screen Again check box to hide the Welcome dialog box. Unless you select this check box, the Welcome dialog box will appear each time you start Approach.

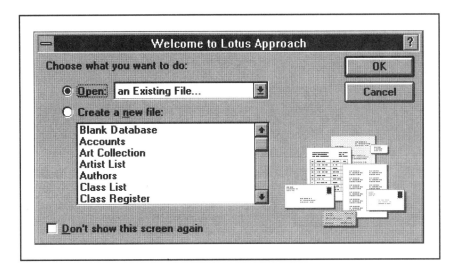

FIGURE 15.1

When you start Approach, you will see the Welcome To Lotus Approach dialog box, which allows you to open or create a database.

N O T E

It is not necessary to display the Welcome To Lotus Approach dialog box in order to create or open a file.

---

4. Click on OK. The New dialog box, shown in Figure 15.2, appears.

5. Type **INVNTORY** in the File Name text box. Approach automatically adds the .DBF file extension.

6. Click on OK. The Creating New Database dialog box, shown in Figure 15.3, appears.

FIGURE 15.2

Type a name for your database file in the File Name text box of the New dialog box, and then click on OK to create a new database file.

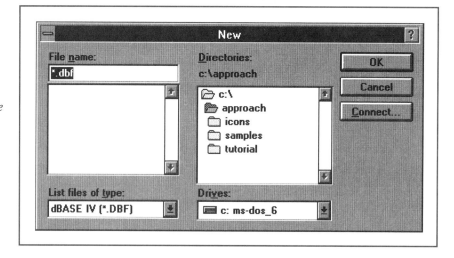

FIGURE 15.3

Add the names of the fields you want for each record in the Creating New Database dialog box.

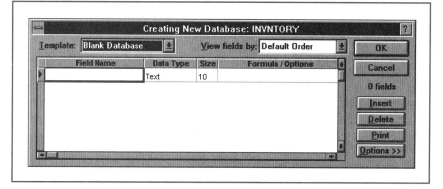

Creating a New Database File

As you can see, Approach encourages you to jump right in and start building the structure of the database. Before you do, though, let's get an idea of what's going on here.

A database is a file that contains many *records*. (A record is all the information in a database about one item. For example, in the INVNTORY.DBF file, a record may consist of a part number, description, supplier, supplier's address, telephone number, etc.) Each record contains several *fields*. (A field is a single named item of information in a record. For example, in the INVNTORY.DBF file, one field may be named "Part No.," and another field may be named "Description.")

NOTE

It is a good idea to break each field down into the smallest amount of information possible so you can use (or not use) each field later when you report on the data. For example, instead of calling a field "Name," break it down into "Title," "First Name," and "Last Name."

Once you decide what kinds of information are necessary for each record, you can build your database by defining the fields. Approach makes this easy with the Creating New Database dialog box, shown in Figure 15.3.

What Types of Fields Can I Use?

Usually each record consists of different kinds of information, such as text, values, dates, etc. Each type of information requires a different

type of field. The following is a description of each of the nine types of fields in Approach:

- A *text* field can consist of any characters you type, such as letters, numbers, symbols, or any combination of those characters. Use text fields for names, descriptions, street addresses, etc. Each text field may contain up to 254 characters, depending on the number you specify when you define the field.

- *Numeric* fields are fields that contain only numbers, such as a price, quantity, or a value used in a calculation.

- Specify a date field as the type in which to store a date.

- Use a *time* field to store a specific time.

- Use a *calculated* field when you want to place the results of a formula in a field. You can use a value in a numeric field, a date, or a time as part of the formula.

- A *memo* field is similar to a text field, but can contain many more characters because it is stored in a file by itself. You cannot sort the data in a memo field.

- Specify a *Boolean* field when you want the field to indicate either yes or no, such as whether a confirmation was sent or a payment was received.

- Use a *PicturePlus* field to store graphic information, such as an employee's photograph.

- A *variable* field is a field that contains one of the above types of data, but the data is stored in your computer's memory rather than in the database. Variable fields are often used in macros.

Adding Fields to Create a Form

Look again at Figure 15.3. There are two ways to add fields to create the new INVNTORY.DBF database:

- Type in a name for each field, specify the type and size of the field, and enter the formula for a calculated field (also known as the hard way).

- Or, create the database using one of Approach's built-in templates (the easy way) and let Approach enter the definition for each field.

NOTE

You can change any of the field definitions, delete unnecessary fields, and insert new fields. See Chapter 17 for additional information about editing fields.

Follow these steps to create a database with a template:

1. Click on the Template drop-down button, scroll through the list until you see Inventory, and then select Inventory to insert the template's fields in the dialog box.

2. Click on Yes to remove the message box, which appears to alert you that the current template's fields will be replaced with the inventory template's fields.

3. Click on OK to create the database. Once you have created a database, the Approach window, shown in Figure 15.4, appears.

FIGURE 15.4

The Approach window appears after you have created (or opened) a database.

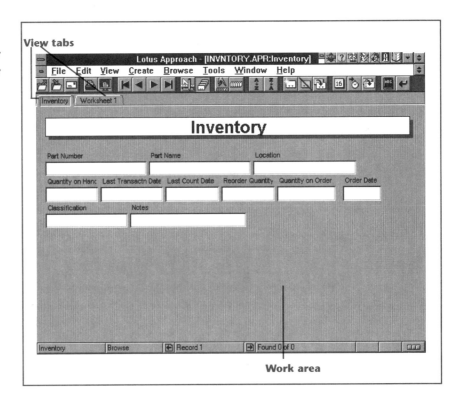

The Approach Window

The Approach window contains a *work area* with two *view tabs*, similar to the worksheet tabs in 1-2-3. The tab of the active view is called Inventory (named after the template you selected in the Creating New Database dialog box). It contains a form with each of the fields in the INVNTORY.DBF file created

earlier. Each field on the form contains its own text box. The data you enter can be placed directly in the appropriate text box.

The other view tab is labeled Worksheet 1. To display the worksheet, just click on the tab. The work area changes, as shown in Figure 15.5.

N O T E

The SmartIcons also change when you switch to the Worksheet 1 view. The new set of SmartIcons, called the Default Sheet set, is used specifically to work on the data in a worksheet.

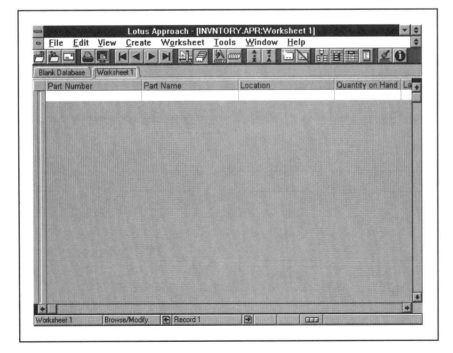

FIGURE 15.5

Click on the Worksheet 1 tab to view the database as a table of information. Each record is a row in the table, and each column contains a field.

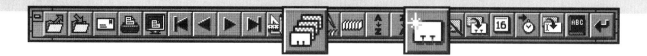

The worksheet displays the fields in the INVNTORY.DBF file in a table. Each record is in one row in the table, and each column contains one field.

Entering Data in a Form

To enter data in the database, you must be in the Browse work environment because that is where you work with the data in the database. Then, just type data in the field text box that contains the insertion point. To move the insertion point to the next text box, press the Tab key. Press Shift+Tab to move to the previous text box.

1. Click on the Inventory view tab to change back to form view.

2. If necessary, click on the Browse button on the Default Browse SmartIcon set.

3. Click on the New Record button. The insertion point appears in the first field text box.

Browse/Modify

N O T E

The Environment button on the status bar displays the current working environment in Approach. When you are entering records in the database, it displays Browse/Modify.

---

4. Type **0001** in the Part Number text box, and then press Tab to move the insertion point to the next field.

5. Type **Weeping cherry tree** in the Part Name text box, and then press Tab.

6. In the Location text box, type **Greenhouse 1**. Press Tab to move to the next field, and then type **0** and press Tab again.

7. To enter a date in the Last Transaction Date text box, type **4/27**, and then press Tab. Approach automatically enters the current year.

8. In the Last Count Date text box, type **2** and press Tab. Approach automatically enters the current month and year.

9. Type **20** and press Tab, and then type **10** and press Tab to enter numbers in the next two fields.

10. Click on the Date button to enter the current date in the Order Date field and move to the next field.

11. Type **Tree** and then press Tab to move to the Notes text box.

12. Type **Mr. Walter Smith needs 6 ASAP**.

13. Click on the Enter button or press ↵ to enter all the information for the first record in the database.

14. Click on the Duplicate Record button to create a second record with the same information in each field.

15. Click on the Enter button or press ↵ to enter the second record.

Don't worry if you accidentally press ↵ while you are entering the data in the fields. Just click on the appropriate text box to place the insertion point in the location where you want to continue entering data.

Managing Your Files

There are two different types of files in Approach. The *database file* contains a definition of the structure of the database and the data you enter. The *Approach file* contains all the forms, worksheets, reports, and letters.

All the work you do in Approach, such as entering and editing data and designing a form, is performed in Approach files. The database files just store the data.

Saving an Approach File

When you save an Approach file, all the views, forms, reports, etc. are saved. (An Approach file can access several different kinds of database files. That is why the database files are separate.)

1. Click on the Save button on the Default Browse SmartIcon set to display the Save Approach File dialog box, shown in Figure 15.6.

FIGURE 15.6

To save an Approach file, click on the Save button on the Default Browse SmartIcon set or choose File ➤ Save Approach File (Ctrl+F) to display the Save Approach File dialog box.

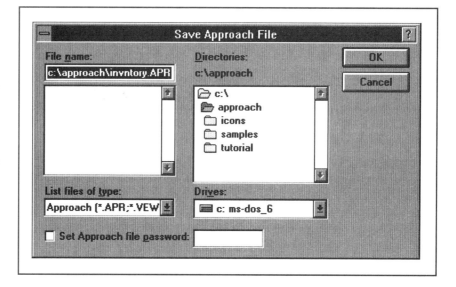

2. Approach suggests a name for the file in the File Name text box. If necessary, type a new name for the file. Approach files are automatically assigned the .APR file extension.

3. Click on OK to save the Approach file.

Once an Approach file has been saved to a named .APR file on your hard disk, you must save it again each time you make a change to the design of the forms, worksheets, reports, letters, etc. in the file. Click on the Save button to save the changes you make to the Approach file without displaying the Save Approach File dialog box again.

Saving a Database File

Each time you press ↵ as you enter the data in a database record, Approach saves the data to a database file on your hard disk. However, you can (and should) make a backup of the database file.

When you make a copy of the database file, you also make a copy of the Approach file that is associated with it. You can follow the steps below to save a named Approach file and its associated database file to a new file name.

1. Insert a formatted disk in either the A: or B: drive.

You must change either the location or the name of the file when making a backup. Otherwise, the backup will simply overwrite the original file on your hard disk.

2. Select File ➤ Save As to display the Save Approach File As dialog box, shown in Figure 15.7.

3. Click on the Drives drop-down button, and then select the letter of the drive into which you inserted the disk. The Directories list box changes to reflect the names of the directories on the disk.

4. If necessary, select the Exact Copy option button in the Databases area of the dialog box to make a copy of both the Approach file and its associated database.

5. Click on OK to save the INVNTORY.APR file. The dialog box is renamed "Save Database As."

6. Click on OK again to save the INVNTORY.DBF file.

FIGURE 15.7

Display the Save Approach File As dialog box to save the Approach file to a new file name, to save the Approach file and its associated database, or to save a copy of the structure of the database.

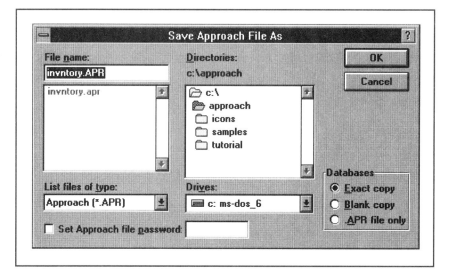

There are two other options you can choose in the Databases area of the dialog box in step 4 above.

- Choose the Blank Copy option button to save only the structure of the database (without the data) when you want to use a database you created as a template for other files.

- To save the Approach file but not its associated data file, choose .APR file only. The new Approach file is still associated with the same database as the original Approach file.

Closing the File

When you are finished working in an Approach file, you can close it and remain in Approach to work on another file.

1. Choose File ➤ Close.

2. If you made any changes to the Approach file, the dialog box shown in Figure 15.8 appears.

 Click on Yes to save the changes made to the Approach file since you last saved it.

 Click on No to close the Approach file without saving the changes you made to it.

 Click on Cancel to return to the current Approach file and its associated database.

FIGURE 15.8

If you change the Approach file before you choose File ➤ Close, a dialog box appears asking if you want to save your changes.

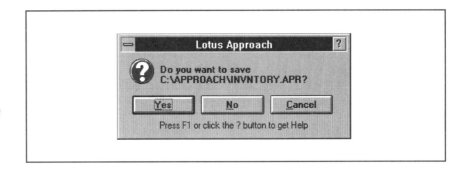

Exiting Approach

When you are finished working in Approach, be sure to exit correctly. When you do, a dialog box similar to the one in Figure 15.8 appears, to remind you to save any changes you made to the Approach file.

1. Double-click on the Control menu box at the left side of Approach's title bar.

2. If you made any changes to the current Approach file, a dialog box similar to that in Figure 15.8 appears.

   Click on Yes to save the Approach file and exit Approach.

   If you click on No, Approach closes without saving changes to the file.

   Click on Cancel to cancel the request to exit if you want to continue working on the current file in Approach.

CHAPTER SIXTEEN

Editing an
Approach File

YOU CAN ADD, delete, or edit the data in an existing Approach file while you are in the Browse environment. When you change to Approach's Design environment, you can also change the structure of the database by adding or deleting fields, or changing the definition of selected fields in each record. Finally, the format of a selected field in an Approach form can be copied from an existing field or changed manually.

Opening an Existing File

When you are ready to add data to or edit the data in a database, open the Approach file.

1. Click on the Start Lotus Approach button on the SmartCenter SmartIcon set to start Lotus Approach.

To quickly reopen one of the last five opened Approach files, select File ➤ Filename.

2. Click on the Open button on the Default Browse SmartIcon set to display the Open dialog box, shown in Figure 16.1.

3. Select INVNTORY.APR in the File Name list box.

4. Click on OK.

The Approach file opens to the form, view, report, etc. that was displayed when you last saved the file.

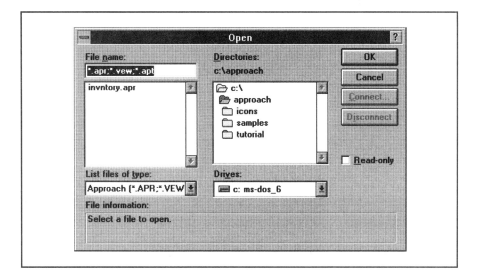

FIGURE 16.1

*The Open dialog box
displays a list of all
your Approach files by
default.*

Opening a New File

To create a new database, open a new file.

1. Select File ➤ New. The New dialog box appears.

2. Type a name for the new file in the File Name text box. For example, type **CUSTOMER**. Approach automatically adds the
.DBF file extension.

3. Click on OK to display the Creating New Database dialog box.

4. Because this database will contain a list of the company's customers, click on the Template drop-down button, scroll through the list, and then select Customers.

5. Click on Yes to remove the message box. The predefined fields in the Customers template appear in the dialog box.

Editing the Field Definitions

The Customers template may not contain the exact field definitions you want for your database. Make changes to the field definitions in the Create New Database dialog box. You can move, insert, replace, or delete the selected field definition while the dialog box is displayed.

To select a field name, just click in its text box. A selected field name appears with a wide, black border around the text box with a triangle pointing to it, as shown in Figure 16.2.

1. Click in the Contact Name field name text box to select the field name, and then type **First Name**.

2. Press Tab twice, type **15** in the Size text box.

3. Press Tab to select the next field name text box, and then click on Insert to insert a blank field definition below the First Name field.

FIGURE 16.2

When a field name is selected in the dialog box, a wide, black border appears around its text box.

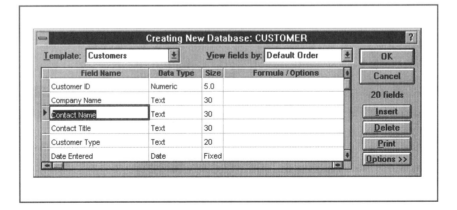

4. Type **Last Name**, and then press Tab twice.

5. Type **15** in the Size text box.

6. Press Tab, and then click on Delete to remove the Contact Title field definition. Each field definition below the deleted field moves up.

7. Scroll down the list of Field Names until the Phone Number field appears.

8. Click on the gray button to the left of the Phone Number field definition to select it, and then position the mouse pointer over the gray button until it appears as a small hand. Drag the button up the list. As you drag, a wide black line appears below each field definition. Release the mouse button when the line is below the Last Name field to drop the selection.

9. Select the Date Entered field name, and then click on the Options button. The Creating New Database dialog box changes, as shown in Figure 16.3.

10. Click on the Creation Date option button to have Approach automatically enter the date a record was added to the database.

11. Select the Date Modified field name, and then click on the Modification Date option button to have Approach change the date automatically each time the record is modified.

FIGURE 16.3

Click on the Options button to change the formula or the options for a field definition.

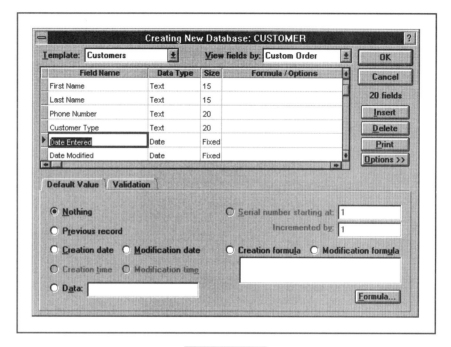

N O T E

To remove an option or formula from the Formula/Options text box, select the field name and then click on the Nothing option button while the options portion of the dialog box is displayed.

12. Click on OK to create the edited database.

A new Approach window appears in the Browse environment. Use the methods described in Chapter 15 to add data to each field, and then press ↵ or click on the Enter button to save the record.

Moving through the Records

The records in a database are numbered consecutively—the first record you enter is record 1, the second is record 2, etc. To edit a record, you must display it on your screen. Once you have entered several records in a database, you can display each one by moving through the records in form view.

Use the following buttons on the Default Browse SmartIcon set to move through the database:

 Click on the First Record button to display the first record in the database.

 Click on the Previous Record button to display the record before the current record.

 Click on the Next Record button to display the record after the current record.

 Click on the Last Record button to display the last record in the database.

You can also move through the database by clicking on one of the following status bar buttons:

 Click on the Previous Record button to display the previous record.

 Click on the Next Record button to display the next record.

 To move to a specific record, click on the Record button to display the Go To Record dialog box, shown below, and then type the number of the record in the text box and click on OK.

Editing a Record

You can edit your data whenever necessary, using the same basic editing techniques you learned for the other SmartSuite applications. In Approach, you can edit the data in either form view or worksheet view when you are in the Browse environment.

To edit a record:

1. Select Window ➤ INVNTORY.APR:Inventory to display the inventory records.

2. If necessary, click on the First Record button to move to the first record of the database.

3. Click in the Location text box, and then select "1." Type **4** to replace the data in the record.

4. Click at the beginning of the Notes field, and then drag to select all the text in the text box. Press Del to delete the note.

5. When you have finished making changes to the data in the record, click on the Enter button to save the changes to the record.

Adding a Field to a Form

Suppose you omitted an important field when you created a database. You can change to the Design environment to edit the form.

> **NOTE**
>
> **Whenever you are working with the structure of the database or the appearance of the data or the form, switch to Approach's Design environment.**

1. With the INVNTORY.APR file displayed in form view, click on the Design button on the Default Browse SmartIcon set to change to the Design environment. If necessary, click on the Drawing Tools button on the Default Design SmartIcon set to display the Design Tools palette, shown in Figure 16.4.

FIGURE 16.4

Use the tools on the Design Tools palette to edit the structure of a database or selected fields in a form.

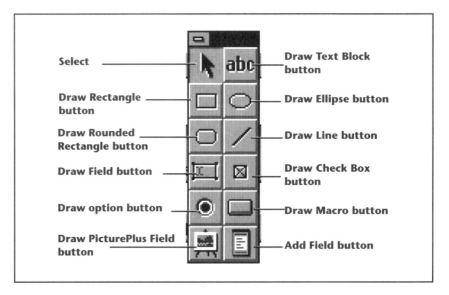

2. In the Design Tools palette, click on the Add Field button to display the Add Field dialog box, shown in Figure 16.5.

3. Click on the Field Definition button to display the Field Definition dialog box, which is similar to the Creating New Database dialog box.

4. Scroll down through the list and click on the Notes field name, and then click on Insert to insert a blank field definition.

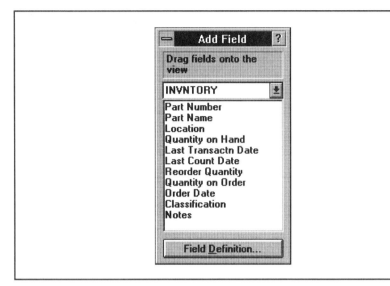

FIGURE 16.5

Display the Add Field dialog box, and then click on the Field Definition button to create a new field definition.

5. Type **Sub-classification** as the field name in the blank text box, and then press Tab twice.

6. Type **20** in the Size text box.

7. Click on OK to return to the Design environment. The Add Field text box displays only the name of the new field.

8. To add the field to the form, select the field name in the Add Field dialog box, and then drag the field into the form.

9. Double-click on the Add Field dialog box's Control menu box to close the dialog box.

Formatting a Field

The field you just added to the form looks just like the other fields in the form. You can apply different styles and properties to a selected field to change its format or copy the format of an existing field.

Changing the Format of a Field

You can change any element of a selected field, such as the format, definition, borders, font, or label using the options in the Settings for dialog box.

1. Select the Part Number field in form view of the INVNTORY.APR file.

2. Click on the Change Properties button on the Default Design SmartIcon Set to display the Settings For dialog box, shown in Figure 16.6.

3. Click on the Label tab, click on the Label Font drop-down button, and select Courier in the list. Then click on the Center button in the Alignment area to center the label over the box.

4. Double-click on the Settings For Control menu box to close the dialog box.

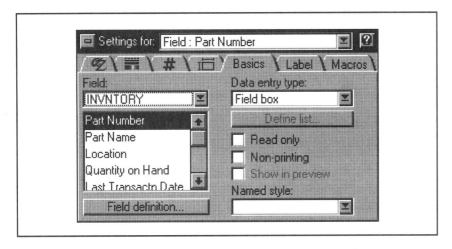

FIGURE 16.6

Each element of a selected field can be changed using options on the tabs in the Settings For dialog box.

Each individual element of the field text boxes can be changed in the Settings For dialog box. Click on the following tabs while a field is selected to change any of the options described below:

On the Basics tab, click on the Field Definition button to display the Field Definition dialog box to insert or delete fields, or change the name or definition of an existing field. To change the name of a field, select the name of the field in the Field list box, and type the new name.

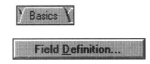

On the Label tab, select a different font, size, color, alignment, or attribute for the selected field's text box label, replace the text of the label, or change the position of the label.

On the Borders and Fill tab, change the size, color, or appearance of the borders of the selected field text box, and the color of the shadow or background (fill) of the box.

On the Font tab, change the font, size, attributes, alignment, or shadow around the characters in the selected field text box.

Copying a Format

Use Fast Format to copy the format (the font, size, and alignment of the label and the characters in the text box) from one field to another.

1. Click on the Show Rulers button on the Default Design Smart-Icon set to display a horizontal ruler below the view tabs and a vertical ruler on the left edge of the screen.

2. Click on the Sub-classification field to select it. A selected field appears with a small, gray handle at each corner of the field text box.

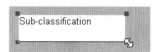

3. To change the size of the field text box, position the mouse pointer over one of the handles, where it appears as a two-headed arrow, and then drag the handle. For example, to increase the size of the box, drag the lower-right handle to the right. Use the ruler to help determine the width of the box.

4. To copy the format of the field text box to the new field, select the Part Number field, and then click on the Fast Format button and click on the Sub-classification field. Then toggle Fast Format off.

5. If necessary, click on the Show Gridlines button to display the form's grid lines (the dots in the background). You may need to select View ➤ Snap To Grid (Ctrl+Y) to have Approach help position the field on the grid in relation to other fields on the form.

6. If necessary, drag the Sub-classification field to a blank area of the form. As you drag, an outline appears around the position of the field.

7. Drag the Notes field to the right side of the last line of the form. Finally, drag the Sub-classification field in front of the Notes field.

N O T E

The Notes field may also need to be repositioned. Just drag it until it appears aligned beside the Sub-classification field.

8. Select the Sub-classification field selected, click on the Underline button on the status bar to underline the characters that are entered in the field's text box.

CHAPTER SEVENTEEN

Managing and Reporting on Your Data

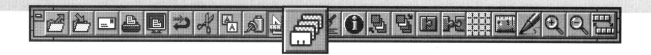

YOUR DATA WON'T be of much use until you can arrange it and report on it. The main reason for placing the data in fields is so you can arrange the records in the database by specifying which field contains the data you need.

Approach can search for and display specific records in a database. Then, you can create different views of the found or arranged data to save in the Approach file.

Finding Specific Data

When you wish to find certain records, switch to the Find environment and request a search by filling out a *find request* (an empty form into which you specify what data you want to find). Approach finds each record in the database that meets the specifications (the *found set*), and displays the found records in the Browse environment.

Defining the Search Criteria

To find all the records in a database that meet certain specifications, define the specifications (the *search criteria*) in the find request. For example, you can find all the records in the INVNTORY.APR file that contain "Tree" in the Classification field, or all records that contain "Annual" in the Sub-classification field.

Click on the Browse button on the Default Design SmartIcon set to switch to the Browse environment, and add some records to the

INVNTORY.APR file so you can practice performing a search. Then follow these steps to display the found set of records:

1. Click on the Find Set button on the Default Browse SmartIcon set. Approach changes to the Find environment and displays a blank form, shown in Figure 17.1.

FIGURE 17.1

In the Find environment, a blank form appears along with the Default Find SmartIcons.

Lotus Approach - [INVNTORY.APR:Inventory]

File   Edit   View   Create   Browse   Tools   Window   Help

Inventory   Worksheet 1

OK   Cancel   Clear Find   Find More

Inventory

Part Number   Part Name   Location

Quantity on Hand   Last Transactn Date   Last Count Date   Reorder Quantity   Quantity on Order   Order Date

Classification   Sub-classification   Notes

Inventory   Find   Records   Found 10 of 10

2. To find all the records in Greenhouse 1, click in the Location text box, and then click on the Equal To button on the Default Find SmartIcon set and type **Greenhouse 1**.

3. Click on OK at the top of the find request.

Approach returns to the Browse environment and displays the first record in the found set. Glance at the status bar to see how many records are in the found set.

> **N O T E**
>
> **To change from displaying the found set back to displaying all the records in the database, click on the All Records button on the Default Browse SmartIcon set.**

Searching for Records Using Multiple Criteria

You can also search for records by specifying search criteria in more than one field text box. For example, to search for all the records that have less than five units on hand and are not trees, follow these steps:

1. Click on the Find Set button on the Default Browse SmartIcon set to switch to the Find environment.

2. Click in the Quantity On Hand field, and then click on the Less Than button on the Default Find SmartIcon set and type **5**.

3. Click in the Classification field, and then click on the Not Equal To button and type **Tree**.

4. Click on OK to display the found set that meets both criteria.

> ### N O T E
>
> To search for records that meet at least one specification in a set of criteria, use an Or search. If the data to search for is in one field, click on the Comma button on the Default Find SmartIcon set to separate the two criteria. If the data is in more than one field, specify the first criterion, click on the Find More button at the top of the find request, and then specify the second criterion. Click on OK to perform the search.

Sorting the Records

By default, records appear in a database in the order in which they were entered. You can sort, or rearrange, the records in a database or in a found set so the records appear to be in a different order. Records can be sorted alphabetically in text fields, numerically in numeric fields, and chronologically in date and time fields.

Sorting on One Field

Use the sorting buttons on the Default Browse SmartIcon set to quickly sort the records in a found set or in the entire database based on the data in a selected field.

- To quickly rearrange the records in a database from A to Z, lowest to highest, or earliest to latest using the data in one field, click in a field box and then click on the Sort Ascending button on the Default Browse SmartIcon set. For example, to sort the records in the INVNTORY.APR file according to the amount in the Quantity On Hand field, click in the box, and then click on the Sort Ascending button.

- To quickly sort the records from Z to A, highest to lowest, or latest to earliest, click in the field on which the data is to be sorted, and then click on the Sort Descending button.

N O T E

To return the sorted records to the default order, click on the All Records button on the Default Browse SmartIcon set.

Sorting on Multiple Fields

Often, you will work with databases that contain records with the same data entered in the field on which you want to sort the database (the *primary sort field*). For example, in a database that includes a mailing list, there may be several records that contain "Smith" in the Last Name field. You can further specify how the database is to be sorted by selecting a secondary sort field (such as the First Name field). The data is first sorted on the value in the primary sort field, then sorted on the value in the secondary sort field.

1. With the INVNTORY.APR file active in the Browse environment, select Browse ➤ Sort ➤ Define (Ctrl+T). The Sort dialog box, shown in Figure 17.2, appears.

FIGURE 17.2

Display the Sort dialog box to define more than one field on which to sort the data.

2. In the Database Fields list box, select the name of the field you want for the primary sort field. For example, scroll down the list and then select Classification.

3. Click on Add to place the highlighted field at the top of the Fields To Sort On list box. If necessary, select Ascending to specify that the field is to be sorted from A to Z.

4. Select Quantity On Hand, and then click on Add. If necessary, select Ascending to specify that the field is to be sorted from lowest to highest.

> **NOTE**
>
> To further specify the sort order, place additional secondary sort fields in the Fields To Sort On list box. The database is sorted according to the order in which the field names are placed in the list box.

5. Click on OK to perform the sort.

The records in the INVNTORY.APR file are sorted alphabetically by the data in the Classification field, then numerically by the data in the Quantity On Hand field. For example, if two records are classified as "Flower," the one with the lower value (6) in the Quantity On Hand field is placed before the record with the higher value (10).

As soon as a field name is selected in the Fields To Sort On list box, several other options become available in the Sort dialog box.

Click on Remove to delete the highlighted field in the Fields To Sort On list box.

To remove all the fields in the Fields To Sort On list box, click on Clear All.

Using the Data in a Database

So far, we have only worked with the data in form view. However, there are other ways to manipulate the data in a database.

Depending on what kind of database is active and how you want to assemble the data, you can create a report, a form letter, or a mailing label. For example, you can create a report on the data in the INVNTORY.APR

file with Report Assistant. Use data in the CUSTOMER.APR file to place the inside address in a form letter and create mailing labels for all the customers in the database.

Use Approach's Report Assistant, Form Letter Assistant, or Mailing Label Assistant to create a different view of your data. Each Assistant displays dialog boxes that allow you to choose the options you want for the view. Let's create a report with Report Assistant as an example.

NOTE

Approach also has a Form Assistant so you can create forms that are different from the default form that appears when you create a new Approach file.

Creating a Report with Report Assistant

Use the data in the INVNTORY.APR file to create a report. You can use either a found set of data or the entire database in the report.

1. Select Create ➤ Report. The Report Assistant dialog box, shown in Figure 17.3, appears.

2. Type a name for the report in the View Name & Title text box. For example, type **Inventory - 1994**.

3. If necessary, click on the SmartMaster Style drop-down button, and then select the name of one of the styles in the list. For example, scroll down the list and then select Executive to apply the style to the report.

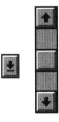

FIGURE 17.3

Display the Report Assistant dialog box to choose the options you want for a report on your data.

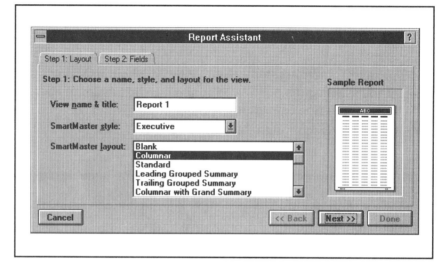

4. Highlight one of the layouts in the SmartMaster layout list box. For this report, we'll use Columnar, which is already selected. An example of the style and layout selected appears in the Sample Report area of the dialog box.

NOTE

If you want to see how other combinations of the SmartMaster styles and layouts appear, just select them before you move to the next set of options. Each time you choose a different style or layout, the changes appear in the Sample Report area.

5. Click on Next to move to the set of options on the next tab of Report Assistant. The Step 2: Fields tab appears in the dialog box, as shown in Figure 17.4.

Next >>

NOTE

Click on Back to move to the previous tab in the Report Assistant dialog box. You can change any option as long as the dialog box is displayed.

<< Back

6. Select the name of the first field you want to include in the report, and then click on Add. For example, select Part Number, and then click on Add to place it in the Fields To Place On View list box. The highlight automatically moves to the next field name in the Database fields list box.

>> Add >>

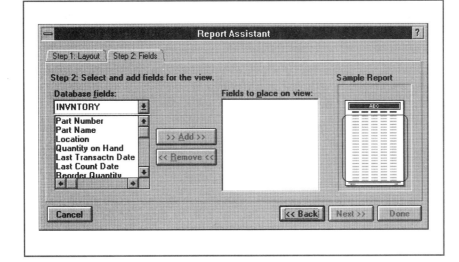

FIGURE 17.4

The next set of options appears on the Step 2 tab in the Report Assistant dialog box.

7. Repeat step 6 for each field you want to include in the report. For example, add the Part Name, Quantity on Hand, Quantity on Order, Classification, and Sub-classification fields to the Fields To Place On View list box.

N O T E

If you decide you do not want one of the fields you added to appear in the report, highlight the name of the field in the Fields To Place On View list box and then click on Remove.

8. Click on Done to compile the report. The report view appears, similar to that in Figure 17.5.

T I P

Click on the Save button on the Default Design SmartIcon set to save the Approach file when you create a new view for the data.

To add or edit data in the report view, click on the Browse button on the Default Design SmartIcon set to change to the Browse environment, and then click on the record you want to edit. The active record appears surrounded by a blue border (on a color monitor). Use the same techniques to edit the data in a field as you used in form view.

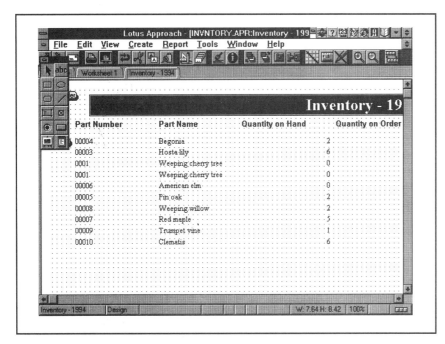

Formatting the Report Text

Any changes you make to the format of the text in the report must be made in the Design environment.

1. Click on the SmartIcons button on the status bar, and then select Default Text in the pop-up list to display the Default Text SmartIcon set.

2. Click on one of the items in the Part Name column to select the entire column, and then click on the Center button on the Default Text SmartIcon set to center the field.

3. Hold down the Ctrl key while you click on the data in any field to place a border around the record that contains the field. Then position the mouse pointer over the lower border until it appears as a two-headed arrow. Drag the border down, just below the text in the next line, to change the report to double-spaced lines.

You can also change the font and size of selected text, add an attribute to a selection, and check the spelling of selected text. Use buttons on the Default Text SmartIcon set and on the status bar to help format the text in a report.

Editing the Structure of the Report

The structure of a report can be changed the same way you changed the structure of the form in Chapter 16. Changes that you make to the structure of the report must be made in the Design environment.

1. Click on the SmartIcons button on the status bar, and then select Default Report in the pop-up list to display the Default Report SmartIcon set.

2. If necessary, click on the Change Style & Properties button on the Default Report SmartIcon set to display the Settings For dialog box for the report, and then choose the settings you want. Double-click on the dialog box's Control box to close it.

NOTE

To display the options for the field names, select the field name whose settings you want to change while the settings for dialog box is diplayed. To display options for the fields, select the data in the field you want to change while the Settings For dialog box is diplayed. The entire column that contains the data in the field is selected, not just the data in the field in one record.

3. To change the width of a column in the report, click in the data to select the column, and then drag the right edge of the selection. For example, select the data in the Quantity On Hand column, and then position the mouse pointer on the right edge of the selection until it appears as a two-headed arrow. Drag the selection to the right to increase the width of the column, or to the left to decrease the width.

Quantity
on Hand

4. To sort the data in the report, select the column that contains the primary data, and then click on the Sort Ascending button. For example, click on the data in the Part Name column, and then click on the Sort Ascending button to sort the displayed records alphabetically.

CHAPTER EIGHTEEN

Printing
Your Data

YOU CAN PRINT the data in a database in any view—forms, worksheets, reports, form letters, or mailing labels, and in the Browse, Preview, or Design environments. Often, a report view is the best choice to print the data when you want the entire database to appear on the printout.

Setting Up the Printer

Before you print the data in one of the views in the INVNTORY.APR file, check to see how your printer is set up. Otherwise, the same printer and options that were selected to print the last Windows document will be used to print the view.

1. Click on the Print button on the Default Report SmartIcon set to display the Print dialog box, shown in Figure 18.1.

Setup...

2. Click on Setup to display the Print Setup dialog box, shown in Figure 18.2.

3. Click on the Portrait option button in the Orientation area of the dialog box.

OK

4. Click on OK to change the printer setup.

Cancel

5. Click on Cancel in the Print dialog box to return to the active view.

Previewing What Will Print

Before you print the active view of the data, preview the view. The preview allows you to see what changes are necessary to the layout or format before you print the active view, and can save you both time and paper.

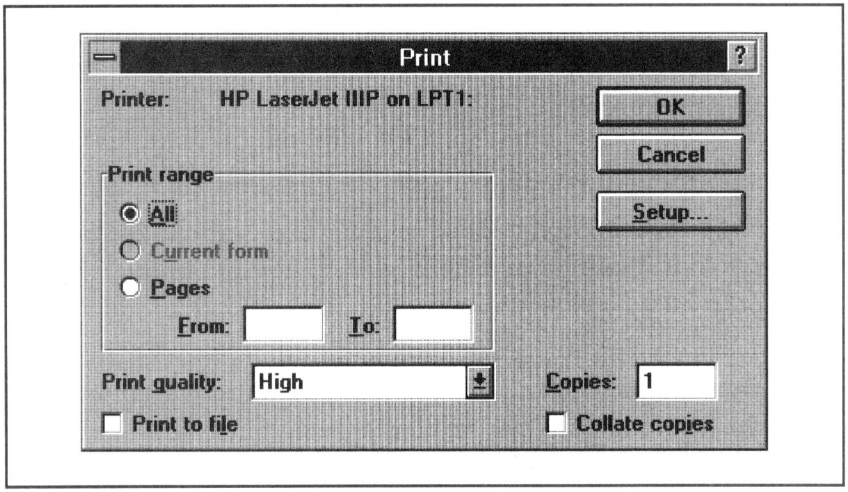

FIGURE 18.1

Click on the Print button to display the Print dialog box, and then click on the Setup button to make sure your printer is correctly set up.

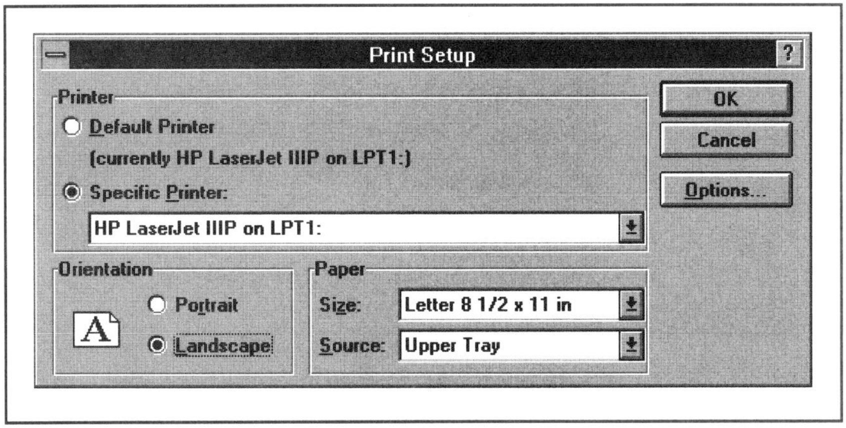

FIGURE 18.2

The page orientation is still set on Landscape. Click on the Portrait option button in the Print Setup dialog box to change the orientation.

You must switch back to the Design environment to make any changes to the format of the active view. Follow these steps to preview and change the appearance of the Inventory - 1994 report:

1. Click on the Preview button on the Default Report SmartIcon set to change to the Preview environment.

2. Move the mouse pointer into the report. It appears as a zoom cursor, a mouse with a magnifying glass attached. Click on the left mouse button to enlarge the page, or on the right mouse button to reduce the page.

3. You may decide that the report view would look better if you made some changes to the format. Click on the Design button on the Default Preview SmartIcon set to switch to the Design environment.

4. Click on the report's title, and then click on the Properties & Style button on the Default Report SmartIcon set to display the Settings For dialog box.

5. Click on the Field Size tab to display the options shown in Figure 18.3.

6. Select the value in the Width text box, and then type **7** and press ↵ to change the width of the report's title.

7. Double-click on the Settings For dialog box's Control menu box to close it.

8. Hold down the Ctrl key while you click on one of the column headings (the report's title is also selected), and then drag the lower border below the first record to insert a blank line under the column headings.

FIGURE 18.3

If necessary, change the width of the title on the Field Size tab of the Settings For dialog box.

9. If necessary, display the Default Design SmartIcon set and click on the Drawing Tools button to display the Drawing Tools pallette.

10. Select the first column heading, and then click on the Draw Text Blocks button on the Design Tools palette. Position the pointer in the selection, and then click before the "N" in "Number" to position the insertion point. Press ↵ to place "Number" on the line below.

N O T E

If the Design Tools palette is in front of the first column heading, move it out of the way. Position the mouse pointer over the palette's title bar, and then drag it to a different location.

11. Drag through "Number" to select it, and then click on the Underline button on the status bar to underline the selection.

12. Click on the Select button on the Design Tools palette, and then repeat steps 9 and 10 to realign and underline each column heading in the report. When you are finished, click again on the Select button.

13. To adjust the width of a column in the report, click on any data in the column to select the column, and then drag the right edge of the selection.

NOTE

You can also display the Default Text SmartIcon set when you want to change the alignment of the data in a selected column or the alignment of a selected column heading with the Align Left, Center, and Align Right buttons.

14. Click on the Preview button to view the report as it will appear when printed.

You may have to switch back and forth several times between the Preview and Design environments until the active view appears just as you want in the Preview environment. Then you are ready to print the view.

Printing the View

You can print all the data in a database, a found set of data, a sorted set of data, or any view in the Approach file. Whatever you want to print

must have been active on your screen when you were last in the Browse environment.

1. With the report active on your screen, click on the Print button on the Default Preview SmartIcon set to display the dialog box shown in Figure 18.1.

2. If necessary, select the number in the Copies text box, and then type the number of copies you want to print.

3. If necessary, select the Collate Copies check box to have Approach print each page of the view before starting on the next copy of the view. When the Collate Copies check box is cleared, the first page is printed the number of times specified in the Copies text box, and then Approach prints the next page (and each succeeding page) the specified number of times.

4. Click on OK to print the report.

5

Freelance
Graphics

CHAPTER NINETEEN

Getting Started with Freelance Graphics

$\mathbf{U}$SE FREELANCE GRAPHICS to quickly create all your presentations. Freelance Graphics comes with over sixty *SmartMasters*, templates you can use to design and lay out each page of your presentation. The SmartMasters also provide the background colors and graphics for your presentation. With Freelance Graphics, you can concentrate on entering your data and let the SmartMasters do the rest of the work.

Starting Freelance Graphics

When you are ready to create a presentation, follow these steps to start Freelance Graphics:

Follow these steps to start Freelance Graphics:

1. Click on the Start Lotus Freelance Graphics button on the SmartCenter SmartIcon set. The first time you run Freelance Graphics, the Welcome To Freelance Graphics! dialog box appears. Click on OK to display the QuickStart window.

2. Select Quit on the menu bar, and then click on Quit QuickStart in the Quit! dialog box. The Welcome To Freelance Graphics dialog box, shown in Figure 19.1, appears.

Creating a New Presentation

The options in the Welcome To Freelance Graphics dialog box let you choose whether to create a new presentation (the default), or open an existing presentation.

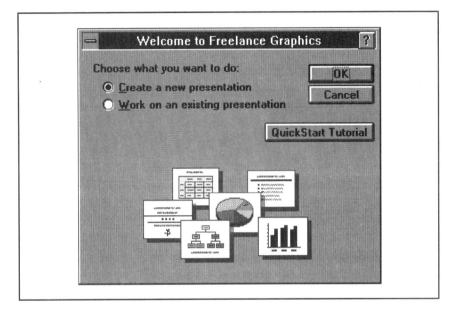

FIGURE 19.1

*Each time you start
Freelance Graphics, the
Welcome To Freelance
Graphics dialog box
appears.*

1. Because the Create A New Presentation option button is already
selected in the Welcome To Freelance Graphics dialog box, just
click on OK to start your presentation. The Choose A Look For
Your Presentation dialog box, shown in Figure 19.2, appears.

2. Scroll through the list box. Notice that an example of the highlighted SmartMaster file in the list box appears in the sample
area of the dialog box. Highlight RAINBOW.MAS in the list box.

3. Click on OK to display the Choose Page Layout dialog box,
shown in Figure 19.3.

FIGURE 19.2

Choose one of Freelance Graphic's SmartMaster sets to provide the background and page layout for your presentation in the Choose A Look For Your Presentation dialog box.

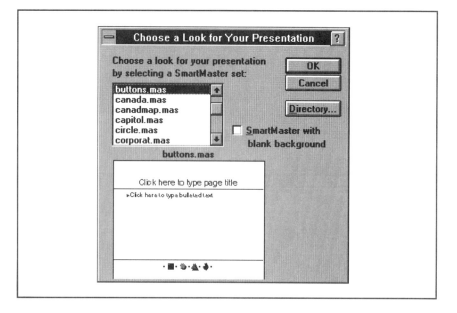

FIGURE 19.3

Select the layout for the first page of your presentation in the Choose Page Layout dialog box.

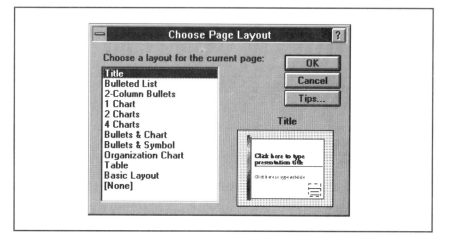

4. By default, "Title" is the selected page layout. Click on OK to create a title page with a rainbow background. The Freelance Graphics window, shown in Figure 19.4, appears.

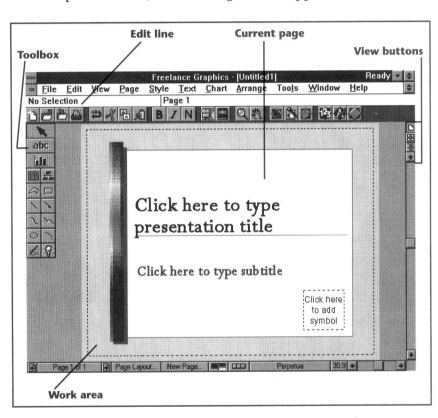

The Freelance Graphics Window

Notice that the Freelance Graphics window is composed of several different parts, labeled in Figure 19.4. The basic window appears just as

do the windows in the other SmartSuite applications, with a title bar, menu bar, SmartIcon set, and interactive status bar. Freelance Graphic's window also contains these elements:

- The *edit line* appears above the Default SmartIcon set. It displays a message telling you what is selected and the name or number of the *current page* of the presentation (the page displayed on your screen).

- Click on one of the tools in the *Toolbox* to draw or insert an object on the current page. For example, choose a tool to draw a text block, an arrow, a circle, or to insert a symbol, chart, or table on the active page.

- The current page is displayed by default in the *work area* of the window when you create a new presentation.

- To display the presentation in a different view, click on one of the *View buttons* on the vertical scroll bar.

Entering the Presentation Data

The SmartMasters help you enter your data by telling you what data should be entered and where to place it on each page of the presentation. All you have to do is choose the page layout for the current page of the presentation, and then follow the instructions on the page.

NOTE

Don't worry if you don't follow all the instructions on a page. The text of the instructions will not appear in your presentation.

Entering Data on the First Page

The first page of a presentation is often the title page, which is why we selected that page layout earlier. It's a good place to start.

1. With the title page current, click on the "Click here to type presentation title" text. A *text block*, a box into which you can enter text on the page, appears.

2. Type **Evergreen National Sales** in the text block, and then click on OK. The title appears on the page surrounded by handles, to indicate that it is selected.

3. Click on the "Click here to type subtitle" text.

4. Type **Regional Sales Report - 1994** in the text block, and then click on OK.

T I P

Click on the Tips button in the text block to display a message box containing a list of tips for entering the text of your presentation with different formats. When you are finished with the list, click on OK to remove the message box.

5. Click on the "Click here to add symbol" block to display the Add Symbol To Page dialog box, shown in Figure 19.5.

FIGURE 19.5

Choose a symbol to place on the page in the Add Symbol To Page dialog box.

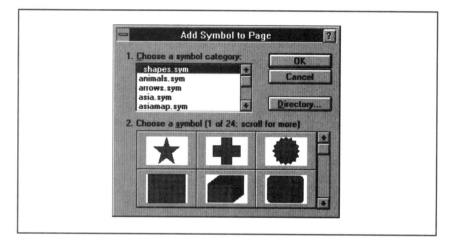

6. Scroll through the Choose A Symbol Category list box, and then select ENVIRONM.SYM as the symbol file. The Choose A Symbol list box changes to display a sample of each symbol in the selected file.

7. Click on the first symbol in the list box and then click on OK to place it on the title page.

Adding a New Page to the Presentation

Each page of a presentation contains only a small amount of data, so you must insert additional pages as they are needed. Each page uses the same background as the one you selected in the SmartMaster file. However, you can choose from a variety of page layouts for each new page.

1. Click on the New Page button on the status bar to add a second page to the presentation. The New Page dialog box, which is similar to the Choose Page Layout dialog box shown in Figure 19.3, appears.

    New Page...

2. Select Bulleted List in the Choose A Page Layout list box, and then click on OK to add a new page to the presentation.

    OK

NOTE

The page number that appears in the Page Name text box is for Freelance Graphics to keep track of the number of pages in the presentation. It will not appear in the presentation.

---

3. Click in the page title area, and then type **First Quarter** in the text block and click on OK.

    OK

4. Click in the bulleted text area, and then type **January Sales - Generally flat**, and press ↵ to begin a new paragraph.

NOTE

Each time you press ↵, the new paragraph is formatted in the same way as the previous paragraph.

---

5. Click on the Indent Bullet button in the text block, and then type **After holidays**. Press ↵, and then type **Bad weather makes planting difficult in many areas**.

N O T E

The text automatically wraps to the next line when it reaches the right edge of the text block. However, the text block expands vertically to accommodate the text for the current page.

---

6. Press ↵, click on the Outdent Bullet button in the text block, and type **February Sales - Picking Up the Pace**.

7. Press ↵ to start a new line, and then type **March - Planting Begins in the South and West**.

8. Click on OK to enter the bulleted list on the second page of the presentation.

Saving the Presentation

In Freelance Graphics, as in any computer program, be sure to save your work often to a file on your disk. The presentation file you save contains all the data you have entered on each page of the presentation, as well as the page layouts and background you selected using the SmartMasters. You must assign a file name to the presentation the first time you save it.

1. Click on the Save button on the Default SmartIcon set. The Save As dialog box, shown in Figure 19.6, appears.

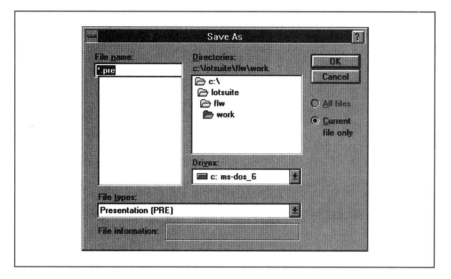

FIGURE 19.6

The Save As dialog box appears the first time you save a presentation.

2. Type **QTR1** in the File Name text box. Freelance Graphics automatically adds the .PRE file extension.

3. Click on OK to save the file.

Once you have named the file, the Save As dialog box will not appear when you click on the Save button to save any changes made to the file.

TIP

To save the file to a new name, select File ➤ Save As to display the Save As dialog box. Type a different name in the File Name text box, and then click on OK.

Closing the File

When you are finished working on a presentation but want to continue working in Freelance Graphics, close the current file to free up some memory in your computer.

1. Select File ➤ Close. If you made any changes to the presentation since you last saved it, the Close Window dialog box, shown in Figure 19.7, appears.

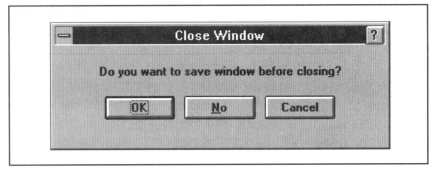

2. Choose one of the buttons described below to tell Freelance Graphics what you want to do.

- Click on OK to save the presentation before closing the file. If you have not saved the presentation to a named file on your disk, the Save As dialog box appears. Type a name for the presentation in the File Name text box, and then click on OK.

- Click on No to close the file without saving the changes you made to it.

- Click on Cancel to keep the presentation file open so you can continue to work on it.

Exiting Freelance Graphics

Close Freelance Graphics when you are finished working on your presentation.

1. Double-click on Freelance Graphics' Control menu box. If you made any changes to an open file since you last saved it, the Exit Freelance dialog box, similar to the Close Window dialog box, shown in Figure 19.7.

2. Choose one of the dialog box buttons described below to tell Freelance Graphics what you want to do.

- Click on OK to save the current presentation, and then exit Freelance Graphics. If any other presentations you have changed are open, the Exit Freelance dialog box reappears. If an open presentation has not been saved to a file, the Save As dialog box appears. Type a name in the File Name text box, and then click on OK.

- Click on No to close the presentation without saving the changes. If you have changed any other file since you last saved it, the dialog box reappears. Otherwise, Freelance Graphics closes, too.

- Click on Cancel to keep Freelance Graphics open and return to the active file.

CHAPTER TWENTY

Editing Your
Presentation

ONE OF THE advantages of using Freelance Graphics to create a presentation is that your presentation is not written in stone. Freelance Graphics makes it easy to edit the data in the presentation or the page layout of the current page, or to change the SmartMaster set you originally selected as the background.

Opening a Presentation File

You can have multiple files open while you are working in Freelance Graphics, depending on the size of each file and the amount of memory available in your computer.

To open a file on your disk:

1. Click on the Open button on the Default SmartIcon set. The Open File dialog box, shown in Figure 20.1, appears.

2. Select the name of the file you want to open in the File Name list box. For example, click on QTR1.PRE. Notice that the size of the file and date it was last saved appear in the File Information area at the bottom of the dialog box.

3. To close the current file on your screen when you open the file, select the Replace Current File check box.

OK 4. Click on OK to open the selected file.

FIGURE 20.1

Display the Open File dialog box when you want to open a presentation file while you are working in Freelance Graphics.

Open File

File name:
*.pre
qtr1.pre

Directories:
c:\lotsuite\flw\work

c:\
lotsuite
flw
work

OK
Cancel

☐ Replace current file

Drives:
c: ms-dos_6

File types:
Presentation (PRE)

File information:

NOTE

When you first start Freelance Graphics, click on the Work On An Existing Presentation option button in the Welcome To Freelance Graphics dialog box and then click on OK to display the Choose Presentation dialog box, similar to the Open File dialog box.

Creating a New File

While you are working in Freelance Graphics, you can create a new presentation file whenever you wish.

1. Select File ➤ New. The Choose A Look For Your Presentation dialog box appears, with the last SmartMaster set you selected still highlighted.

2. Select the name of the SmartMaster set you want to use as the background for the new presentation in the list box that contains the names of the SmartMaster files. For example, select SHIP.MAS. Or, to use a SmartMaster with a blank background for your presentation, select the SmartMaster With Blank Background check box.

3. Click on OK to open a new presentation with the SHIP.MAS SmartMaster as the background. The current page on the screen changes to a blue background, and the Choose Page Layout dialog box appears.

4. Because "Title" is already selected in the Choose A Layout For The Current Page list box, just click on OK to place the title page layout on the current page.

Now you can add the title page data for a second presentation.

Editing a Presentation

You can change virtually everything in a presentation. For example, you can insert additional pages to add text to the presentation, delete

existing text and characters in the presentation, or change the format of selected text. You can also change the presentation's background at any time or add a symbol to the current page. In fact, you can try out all kinds of different looks for your presentation.

T I P

To reverse the last change you made to a presentation, click on the Undo button on the Default SmartIcon set.

Changing the Text

Use all the regular editing methods to change existing text in a presentation.

1. Select Window ➤ QTR1.PRE to make the First Quarter presentation current. If necessary, click on the Next Page button on the status bar to make page 2 the current page.

2. Click on the bulleted list to select the text block that contains it. Then click just before "March" to position the insertion point, and drag through the entire "March" item in the list.

3. Click on the Cut button on the Default SmartIcon set to place a copy of the text in the Clipboard.

4. Click on the New Page button on the status bar. Highlight Bullets & Chart in the Choose A Page Layout list box, and then click on OK to insert the new page after page 2.

5. Click in the bulleted text area, and then click on the Paste button to place the Clipboard's contents in the text block on the new page.

6. Click on OK to place the text on the new page.

7. Click in the page title area of the new page. Then type **March Sales on the Rise** and click on OK.

8. Click on the Previous Page button on the status bar to make page 2 current. Then click just after the last bullet in the selected bulleted list, press Backspace to delete the bullet and the blank line, and click on OK.

Page 1 of 4

Formatting the Text

The text on a page of your presentation appears in the style that is assigned to the text block that contains it. You can change the format of

all of the text in the text block when the text block is selected. Or, you can change the format of selected text within a selected text block.

N O T E

To change the display of the current page while you are editing the presentation, click on the Zoom Page button on the Default SmartIcon set and then click in the area you want to magnify. To move the magnified page to display another area, click on the Move Page button, and then drag the page until the area you want to see is displayed. To zoom out on the magnified page, click on the Zoom Page button, and then hold down the Shift key while you click on the magnified page.

---

1. Click on the Previous Page button on the status bar to make the title page of the presentation current.

2. Click on the title to select the text block. Handles appear around a selected text block.

3. Click on the Font button on the status bar, and then select Brittanic Bold in the pop-up list.

Perpetua

4. Click on the Point Size button on the status bar, and then select 42 in the pop-up list.

54.9

5. Click in the subtitle text block to select it, and then click before "Regional" to position the insertion point.

6. Drag through "Regional" to highlight it. Then select Text ➤ Font to display the Font dialog box, shown in Figure 20.2.

FIGURE 20.2

To change the color of selected text in a presentation, display the Font dialog box.

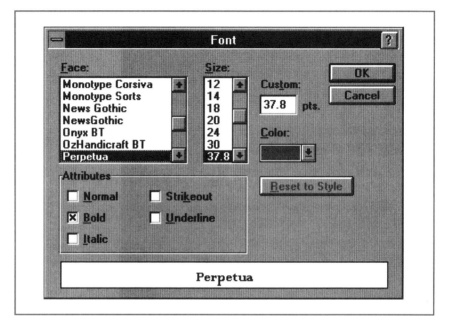

7. Click on the Color drop-down button to display the color palette, and select a different color for the text.

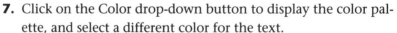

8. Click on OK to change the color of the selected text.

9. Click on OK again to confirm that you want to change the selection in the text block.

Choose one of the following buttons on the Default SmartIcon set to apply or remove an attribute to selected text or the text in a selected text block:

Click on the Bold button to toggle the bold attribute on or off for selected text.

Click on the Italics button to toggle the italics attribute on or off for selected text.

Click on the Underline button to toggle the Underline attribute on or off for selected text.

Changing the Format of the Page

You can change the background of each page in the presentation, or change the layout of the current page at any time.

- To change the background, select a different SmartMaster set. Select Style ➤ Choose SmartMaster Set to display the Choose SmartMaster Set dialog box. Then select the name of the file that contains the SmartMaster set and click on OK.

- To insert a new page layout for the current page, click on the Page Layout button on the status bar to display the Choose Page Layout dialog box. Then select the name of the layout you want to insert and click on OK.

Adding Symbols to a Page

Each SmartMaster set contains two page layouts that contain a *graphics block*, an area into which a picture can be placed, to be used specifically for adding a symbol—the Title and the Bullets & Symbol page layouts. In Chapter 19, you saw how to add a symbol to the title page by clicking on the "Click here to add symbol" block. However, you can add symbols to any page in a presentation to enhance a particular page.

Inserting a Symbol

To place a symbol on a page that does not contain a graphics block:

1. Click on the Next Page button on the status bar to make page 2 of the presentation current.

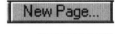

2. Click on the New Page button on the status bar to display the New Page dialog box. Select Bulleted List in the Choose A Page Layout list box and click on OK to add a new page after page 2.

3. Click on the Add Symbol button on the Toolbox. The Add Symbol To Page dialog box appears.

4. Select the type of symbol you want in the Choose A Symbol Category list box and click on the picture of the symbol in the Choose A Symbol list box. For example, select FINANCE.SYM to display the financial symbols, and then click on the picture of the safe. Click on OK to insert the symbol on the page. The symbol appears selected, surrounded by handles.

Moving and Sizing a Symbol

When you insert a symbol on a page, it may not appear in the position or size in which you want it to be. You can move or change the size of a selected symbol.

To select a symbol, just click on it. Then use any of the following methods to move or size the symbol:

- To move a symbol, drag it to a new position on the page. For example, drag the safe to the center of page 3. An outline of the

graphics box that contains the symbol appears as you drag. Release the mouse button when the outline appears in the position in which you want it to be.

- To change the size of a symbol proportionally, position the mouse pointer on one of the corner handles until it appears as a two-headed arrow. Then drag away from the symbol to make it larger, or drag toward the symbol to make it smaller. For example, drag one of the corner handles toward the safe to make it smaller.

- To change the symbol's height, drag either of the handles at the center of the top or bottom of the graphics block.

- To change the symbol's width, drag either of the handles at the center of the left or right side of the graphics block.

You can also add text to a page that contains a symbol. For example, click in the bulleted text block to add a bulleted item on the same page as the symbol.

NOTE

To add a text block to a page that does not already have one (for example, a page with the Blank page layout), click on the Text Block button in the Toolbox, move the mouse pointer to the position on the page at which you want to place a text block, and then drag down and to the right to form a rectangle. When you release the mouse button, the text block appears, all ready for you to enter your text.

abc

CHAPTER TWENTY-ONE

Changing the View of the Presentation

UNTIL NOW, you have been working in Current Page view to add and edit the data in the presentation. In Current Page view, each individual page was placed in the presentation with its own set of data and/or graphics.

However, there are other ways you can work on your presentation. For example, you can switch to Page Sorter view to change the order of the pages, or to Outline view to see and work on only the text portion of the presentation.

Changing the Order of the Pages

Once you have placed all the data on each page in a presentation, click on the Page Sorter button, found in the View buttons at the top of the vertical scroll bar, to switch to Page Sorter view. Each page in the presentation appears reduced on your screen with its title below the page, so you can check to make sure that the pages appear in the order in which you want them presented. While you are in Page Sorter view, you can change the order of the pages or change the title of a selected page.

1. Click on the Page Sorter button, located in the View buttons at the top of the vertical scroll bar. The view changes, as shown in Figure 21.1.

N O T E

To select a page while you are in Page Sorter view, click on the page. To select multiple pages, hold down the Shift key while you click on the pages.

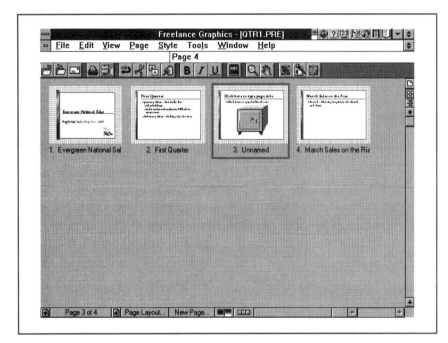

FIGURE 21.1

When you change to Page Sorter view, each page in the presentation appears reduced on your screen.

2. Page 3, which was the current page when you switched to Page Sorter view, is selected on your screen—it appears with a gray box around both the page and the name of the page. To change the name (or title) of the page in Page Sorter view, click in the title box on the edit line and drag through the characters. Then type **Time for Improvement** in the title box and click on the Confirm box.

N O T E

Although the name (or title) of the page is changed in Page
Sorter view, it is not actually changed in the presentation. You
must change the text of the presentation in either Current
Page or Outliner view, which is explained later in this chapter.

3. To change the order of the pages, drag page 3 to the right side of
page 4. As you drag, an outline appears around the position of the
page. When the page is correctly positioned beside page 4, a
gray vertical bar appears. Release the mouse button to move
page 3 to the new position.

N O T E

To return to Current Page view, click on the Current Page button, located in the View buttons on the vertical scroll bar.

Changing to Outliner View

Switch to Outliner view to help you organize the text in your presentation. You can also create the text portion of a presentation in Outliner
view by switching to Outliner view right after you choose the layout for
the first page of the presentation if you want to quickly place your ideas
"on paper." After the text is complete, you can work with the SmartMaster sets and page layouts to redesign the presentation.

To switch to Outliner view, click on the Outliner button, located in the View buttons on the vertical scroll bar. In Outliner view, shown in Figure 21.2, the text on each page of the presentation appears on lined paper on your screen, and the Outliner buttons appear on a button bar above the paper.

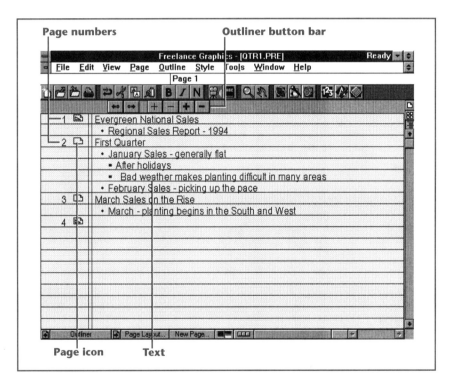

FIGURE 21.2

Switch to Outliner view to create or display the text portion of a presentation. In Outliner view, each line of text after the title of the page appears as a bulleted list item.

The Outliner window is made up of several elements:

- *Page numbers* appear in the first column on the paper.

- Each page number is followed by a *page icon,* which indicates what the page contains. For example, in Figure 21.2, the page 1 icon indicates that the title page contains a symbol, and the page 2 icon indicates that the second page contains only text.

- The *text* on each page appears just after the double vertical line on the paper. Each page appears in Bulleted page layout in Outliner view. (Notice that page 4 doesn't contain any text right now.)

- The Outliner buttons appear on a *button bar* above the paper. They are used to promote or demote, or hide or display text in the presentation.

- The *Page Number button* on the status bar changes to indicate that you are in Outliner view.

Editing the Presentation Text

Outliner view makes it easy to create or edit the text portion of your presentation. You can add, replace, or delete text in the presentation. You can also move or copy existing text to a different page.

- To add text to the title page of the presentation, click after 1994 in the subtitle text and press ↵. Notice the new paragraph appears at the same *level* as the previous paragraph. (An outline level is the position of text in relation to the surrounding text in the outline.) Type **National Sales By Quarter** to insert additional text on the page.

> ### N O T E
>
> **You must also type the title text for page 4. Click beside its icon, and then type Time for Improvement to enter the title into the presentation.**

- To delete a bulleted item, click on the bullet to select the item, and then press Del. A selected item appears with a blue border around it.

- To replace text in the outline, drag through the text to highlight it, and then type new text. For example, drag through "Generally flat" on the second page, and type **Usually Very Slow**.

- To move a bulleted item, point to the bullet, and then drag the item. As you drag, the mouse pointer turns into a move page pointer (a large triangle pointing to the right) and a horizontal bar appears in the current position of the item. When the bar appears where you want to place the item, release the mouse button. For example, point to the second indented bullet on page 2, and then drag the item below the title on page 3 and release the mouse button. Notice that the item retains its original outline level.

- You can also use the Cut button on the Default SmartIcon set to move selected text or a selected item. For example, select the ti-tle of page 2, "First Quarter," and click on the Cut button. Click on the line beside the second bulleted item on page 1, and click on the Paste button to move the title.

- To copy text, drag through the text to select it, and then click on the Copy button on the Default SmartIcon set. For example, select "March Sales on the Rise," and then click on the Copy button. Now click beside the page 2 icon, and click on the Paste button to paste a copy of the selection.

- To return the title of the page to its original position, select "First Quarter," and click on the Cut button. Then select the cur-rent page 2 title, and click on the Paste button to replace the text in the presentation.

- To move an item up (to the left) one outline level, select the item and click on the Promote button on the Outliner button bar. For example, to promote the bulleted item "After holidays" on page 2, click on the bullet to select the item, and then click on the Promote button. The item moves up (left) one outline level.

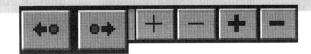

- To move an item down (to the right) one outline level, select the item and then click on the Demote button on the Outliner button bar. For example, with "After holidays" still selected, click on the Demote button to move it one level down (to the right) in the outline.

Go ahead and move the "Bad weather makes planting difficult in many areas" item back to page 2, to return the item to its correct position.

Editing the Pages in a Presentation

You can also move, add, or delete pages in the presentation.

- To move a page, drag the page icon to a different position. As you drag, the move page pointer appears and a horizontal bar is displayed to indicate the current location of the selected page. For example, drag the page 3 icon to page 4 to move the entire page.

- To add a new page, promote the outline level until it becomes a new page. For example, click after the title on page 3 and press ↵ to start a new paragraph on the page. Now click on the Promote button on the Outliner button bar to insert a blank page between pages 3 and 4.

- To delete a page, click on the page's title line, and then click on the Demote button on the Outliner button bar. For example, click on the page 2 title line, and then click on the Demote button. The page is deleted, and the text is automatically placed on the page before it. Notice that all the pages after the deleted page are renumbered.

Controlling What Is Displayed

If you are working on a long presentation in Outliner view, you can control how much of the outline is displayed. You can also switch back and forth between Outliner and Current Page views as you work to fine tune your presentation.

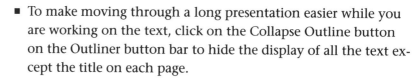

- To make moving through a long presentation easier while you are working on the text, click on the Collapse Outline button on the Outliner button bar to hide the display of all the text except the title on each page.

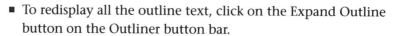

- To redisplay all the outline text, click on the Expand Outline button on the Outliner button bar.

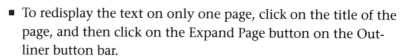

- To redisplay the text on only one page, click on the title of the page, and then click on the Expand Page button on the Outliner button bar.

- To hide the text except for the title on only one page, click anywhere in the text of the page, and then click on the Collapse Page button on the Outliner button bar.

- To display a page in Current Page view, click anywhere in the text of the page, and then click on the Current Page button, found in the View buttons at the top of the vertical scroll bar.

- To return to Outliner view, click on the Outliner button in the View buttons at the top of the vertical scroll bar.

CHAPTER TWENTY-TWO

Displaying a Presentation

ONCE YOU HAVE created a presentation, you can display it either on printed pages or as a show on your computer screen. You can even create your own notes for each page of the presentation.

Creating Notes for the Speaker

You can use Freelance Graphic's Speaker Notes feature to create notes for the current page in Current Page view or for the selected page in Page Sorter view. The speaker notes for a page can include reminders and information to support the data on the page (such as the source of the data).

Each page for which you create speaker notes displays the Speaker Notes icon. The Speaker Notes icon appears on the left of the page (below the Toolbox) in Current Page view, or below the page (beside the page name) in Page Sorter view.

To create speaker notes for a page:

1. Click on the Current Page button or the Page Sorter button, found in the View buttons above the vertical scroll bar, to switch to either Current Page or Page Sorter view.

2. If necessary, click on the Previous Page or Next Page button on the status bar to select page 2 on which to add speaker notes.

3. Select Page ➤ Speaker Notes. The Speaker Note—*Page Name* (First Quarter, in this case) dialog box, shown in Figure 22.1, appears.

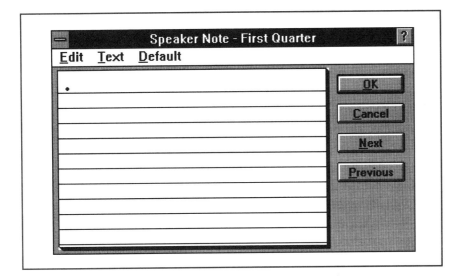

FIGURE 22.1

Display the Speaker Note–Page Name dialog box to create a note for the speaker on the current page of the presentation.

4. Type the text on the note card in the dialog box. For example, type **First Quarter sales for January totaled $2482.00**. Notice how the text automatically wraps to the next line when the insertion point reaches the right edge of the note card.

5. Press ↵ to start a new paragraph. Each paragraph on the note card appears in a bulleted list.

6. Type **February first quarter total–$3223.00**.

7. Click on OK to attach the speaker notes to the current page.

To redisplay the Speaker Note—*Page Name* dialog box for a page, click on the Speaker Note icon in Current Page or Page Sorter view.

You can add, delete, or replace text on the note card using the regular text editing methods. To cut, copy, or paste a selection, use the commands on the Edit menu in the Speaker Note dialog box. To change the

font or apply an attribute to selected text on the note card, use the commands on the Text menu in the Speaker Note dialog box.

Printing the Presentation

If you have a color printer, the presentation will be printed in color. Of course, if you have a black and white printer, the colors won't be printed.

To see how the presentation will appear when printed with a black and white printer, click on the Color button on the status bar. Toggle the Color button to redisplay the presentation in color.

When you are ready to print the presentation, follow these steps:

1. Click on the Print button on the Default SmartIcon set. The Print File dialog box, shown in Figure 22.2, appears.

2. If necessary, type a new number in the Number Of Copies text box in the Print area. Or, to print a range of pages, type the beginning page in the From Page text box and the last page in the To text box.

- To print several pages of the presentation that are not in a range, click on the Page Sorter button in the View buttons and select each page you want to print. Then, click on the Print button and select the Selected Pages Only check box.

- To print only one page, click on the Current Page button in the View buttons and click on the Previous Page or Next Page button on the status bar to make the page you want

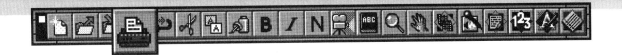

FIGURE 22.2

Display the Print File dialog box to print the presentation, speaker notes, audience notes, handouts, or outline.

to print current. Then, click on the Print button and select the Current Page Only check box to print the current page.

3. In the Format area of the dialog box, click on one of the option buttons described below.

> **Full page** Choose this option to print each entire page you specified in step 2.

> **Speaker notes** Choose this option to print the speaker notes for the pages specified in step 2 below a small picture of the entire page.

Audience notes Choose this option to print a small picture of the specified page, with room for the members of the audience to write their own notes below it.

Handouts Choose this option and then select the check box to specify whether you want to print 2, 4, or 6 miniature presentation pages on a single page to distribute to the audience.

4. Click on the Print button to print the presentation.

N O T E

To print only the text of the presentation, click on the Outliner button above the vertical scroll bar before you click on the Print button on the Default SmartIcon set. Then click on the Outline option button in the Format area of the Print File dialog box, and click on the Print button.

Running a Screen Show

You can also create a screen show to display each page of the presentation on your computer screen. Use a screen show to review your presentation on-screen before you present it, or to present the screen show for an audience.

To display your presentation as a screen show:

1. Select File ➤ Printer Setup to display the Printer Setup dialog box, shown in Figure 22.3.

FIGURE 22.3

Display the Printer Setup dialog box and choose the Optimize For Screen Show option button to print the presentation to the screen rather than to the printer.

Printer Setup

○ Optimize for screen show
● Printers:

Genigraphics® Driver on GENI:
HP LaserJet IIIP on LPT1:
Quick Link II Fax on FAX/MODEM

☐ Set margins for slides

OK
Cancel
Setup...

---

2. Click on the Optimize For Screen Show option button and click on OK to print the presentation to the screen rather than to the printer.

3. Click on the Screen Show button on the Default SmartIcon set to run the presentation as a screen show. The screen show always starts on page 1 of the presentation.

4. To advance to the next page, press ↵.

NOTE

As you are running the screen show, point to important data on each page with your mouse pointer.

5. Repeat step 4 until you reach the end of the presentation. You are automatically returned to the view in which the presentation was displayed before you ran the screen show.

Adding Special Effects to the Screen Show

You can jazz up a screen show presentation by specifying how long each page appears on the screen and how each succeeding page replaces the previous page.

> ### N O T E
> See your Freelance Graphics documentation for information on adding sound to a presentation and using your mouse to draw on the current page.

1. While you are in Current Page or Page Sorter view, select View ➤ Screen Show ➤ Edit Effects. The Edit Screen Show dialog box, shown in Figure 22.4, appears.

2. In the Choose A Page area, click on the Previous Page or Next Page button until the page to which you want to apply special effects appears. For example, click on the Previous Page button until page 1 is displayed.

3. In the Choose An Effect list box, select the name of the replacement effect you want to use on the page. For example, select Checkerboard.

4. Click on Preview Page to see how the replacement effect appears. If necessary, choose a different replacement effect. Press ↵ to return to the Edit Screen Show dialog box.

5. In the Advance Screen Show area, click on the Automatically option button. Then, type the number of seconds you want each page to appear on your screen in the Display Page For Seconds text box. For example, drag through 3, the default, and type 5.

6. Click on OK to confirm the special effects for the screen show and return to the presentation.

7. Click on the Screen Show button on the Default SmartIcon set to run the screen show.

Notice that each page of the presentation advances automatically. However, you assigned a special effect to only the first page of the screen show presentation. If you wish, repeat steps 1 through 5 for the next four pages of the presentation, and then click on OK to assign special effects to the entire presentation.

6

Organizer

CHAPTER TWENTY-THREE

Creating a Datebook
with Organizer

USE ORGANIZER TO manage your day-to-day life. You can enter all of your appointments and set an alarm to remind you of them when they approach. You can even keep an electronic Rolodex of the names and addresses of everyone you know.

Starting Organizer

When you are ready to start Organizer, just click on the Start Lotus Organizer button on the SmartCenter SmartIcon set. The Organizer window, shown in Figure 23.1, appears.

The Organizer Window

Notice that Organizer appears as an electronic datebook, with the same sections you might have in a paper datebook. There is even an area for you to enter the name of the person to whom the datebook belongs. One major difference between Organizer and a paper datebook is that with Organizer, you can create as many new datebooks as you want.

The Organizer window is composed of several elements, shown in Figure 23.1:

- The *Toolbox* contains buttons you can click on to access Organizer commands or functions.

- The time set in your computer is displayed in the *clock* below the Toolbox.

- The date set in your computer is displayed on the *date calendar* below the clock.

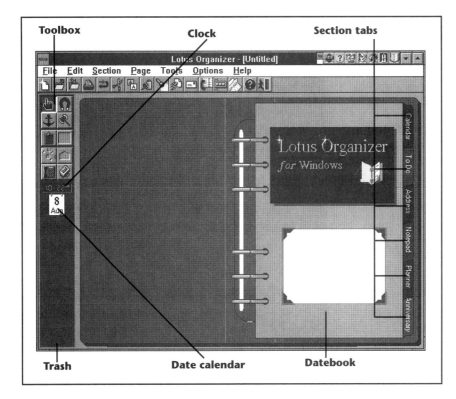

FIGURE 23.1

The Organizer window appears whenever you start Organizer.

- To delete an item in Organizer, just drag it to the *trash*.

- Organizer's *datebook* appears in the window. The datebook has *section tabs* to separate each section. Click on the section tab you want to open to move directly to its first page.

- The *datebook cover* is the gray area around the notebook.

N O T E

To display the end of the datebook, click on its inside-back cover. To return to the beginning of the datebook, click on its inside-front cover.

The first page of the datebook contains the title of the application and an area that looks like a desk pad. Click in the desk pad and type the text that indicates a title for the datebook. For example, type **Appointments for Evergreen Nursery and Landscaping, Inc**. When the insertion point reaches the right edge of the desk pad, the text automatically wraps to the next line. Press ↵ to begin a new line of text on the desk pad.

Opening the Calendar

To enter an appointment in the datebook's Calendar section, first display the date for the appointment.

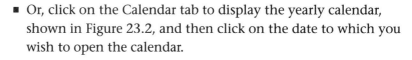

- To quickly move to the current date, click on the date calendar.

- Or, click on the Calendar tab to display the yearly calendar, shown in Figure 23.2, and then click on the date to which you wish to open the calendar.

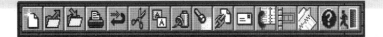

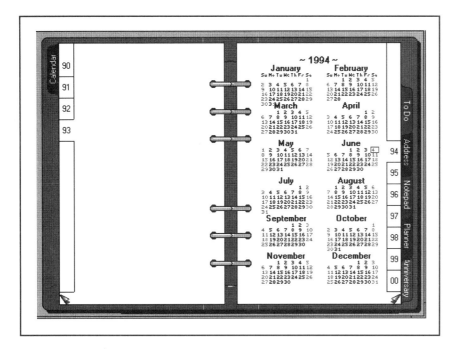

FIGURE 23.2

The calendar for the whole year appears when you click on the Calendar tab.

No matter how you specify the date to which to open the calendar, by default the calendar opens to display the entire week that contains that date. To change the display of the calendar, click on one of the View buttons that appears under the date calendar when you open the calendar.

Click on the Two Days button to display the specified date and one day either before or after it.

Click on the Work Week button to display the days of the work week that include the specified date (the default).

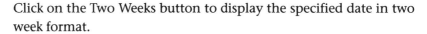

 Click on the Two Weeks button to display the specified date in two week format.

 Click on the One Week button to return to the default one-week calendar display.

 To move to a different page in the calendar, or any section of the notebook, point to the turned-up corner at the lower-left side or lower-right side of the page. When the mouse pointer changes into a pointing hand, click on the corner of the page to turn to the next (or the previous) page.

Entering Appointments in the Calendar

When the date in which you want to enter an appointment is displayed, click on it to activate the date. The active date (shown below) appears with a list of times.

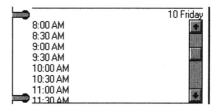

1. Click on the time for which you want to enter the appointment in the list. For example, click on 10:00 AM to activate it. The

insertion point appears in the selected time's appointment window (shown below).

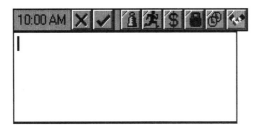

2. Type a description of the appointment in the appointment window. For example, type **Meeting with Grows-A-Lot sales rep**.

3. Click on the Confirm button at the top of the appointment window to place the appointment in the calendar.

NOTE

To edit the appointment description, just click on the time to activate it. Then use the regular editing methods to insert, replace, or delete the text. When you are finished, click on the Confirm button at the top of the appointment window to enter your changes.

You can also change the time of a selected appointment:

Drag the center of the TimeTracker icon to adjust the time for the appointment. For example, drag 1:00 down to make the appointment later. The time at the top of the icon indicates the new time for the

appointment. Click on the Confirm button above the appointment window to enter the change in the appointment.

Setting an Alarm

To have Organizer remind you that an appointment is approaching:

1. Click on an appointment you entered in the calendar to activate it.

2. Click on the Alarm button at the top of the appointment window to display the Alarm dialog box, shown in Figure 23.3.

FIGURE 23.3

Display the Alarm dialog box to set an alarm for the active time.

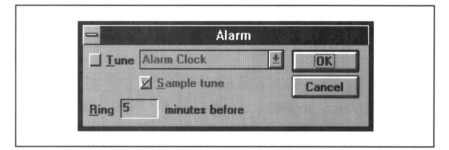

3. Select the Tune check box to make the alarm play a tune, and then click on the drop-down button and select the name of the tune to play when the alarm goes off. The tune you select will play while the dialog box is displayed if the Sample Tune check box is selected (the default).

4. Click on OK to set the alarm for the active time.

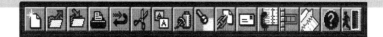

5. Click on the Confirm button at the top of the appointment window to save the alarm set for the appointment.

6. Five minutes before the time set, the tune plays and a message box appears. Click on OK to acknowledge the message.

Adding Items to the To Do List

Use Organizer's To Do section to keep a list of items on an up-to-date "to do" list.

1. Click on the To Do tab to display the first page of that section. Then, click anywhere on the page or on the New Entry button in the Toolbox to display the To Do dialog box, shown in Figure 23.4.

FIGURE 23.4

To add an item to the To Do list, enter the item and the date for it in the To Do dialog box.

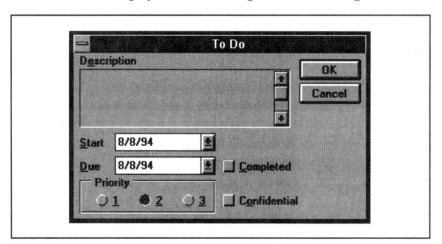

2. Type **Prepare new sales presentation for Marketing Dept.** in the Description text box.

3. Click on the Start drop-down button to display a calendar for the current month. Then click on the date on which you want to start the task.

NOTE

If you need to display a different month on the calendar, click on the Previous icon on the calendar to display the previous month or the Next icon to display the next month.

4. Repeat step 3 to enter a date in the Due text box.

5. Click on OK to enter the item in the To Do list.

N O T E

To have the items in the To Do list automatically placed in your Calendar, select Options ➤ Calendar to display the Calendar Options dialog box, click on the Show button to display the Calendar Options (Show) dialog box, and then click on To Do in the Show Entries From list box. Click on OK in the Calendar Options (Show) dialog box, and again in the Calendar Options dialog box to confirm placing the list in the Calendar.

When you have completed the task, drag it to the trash from either the Calendar or the To Do page. Organizer will quickly delete it.

Entering Addresses in the Address Book

Use Organizer's Address section to keep an alphabetical list of people and companies. The Address section is a database of names, addresses, telephone numbers, and even notes, such as the date the person was last contacted or the names of his or her children, for each record.

1. Click on the Address tab to activate the first page of the section.

2. Type a title in the Title field. For example, type **Mr.**

3. Press Tab to move to the First Name field, and then type **Walter**.

4. Press Tab again to highlight the Last Name field, and then type **Smith**. The characters you enter in the Last Name field are the

ones Organizer uses to alphabetize the entries in the Address section.

5. Press Tab to highlight the Position field, and then type **Homeowner**.

6. Press Tab twice, once to bypass the Company Name field, and again to highlight the Address field. Then type **8214 Apple-tree Avenue** and press ↵ to start a new line. Type **Atlanta, GA**, and then press Tab to move to the Zip field. Type **30301**.

7. Press Tab, and then type **Business** in the Type field.

8. Click on Insert to place the first record in the Address section.

9. To add another record, click on the New Entry button in the Toolbox to redisplay the form. Then repeat steps 2 through 8 to enter the data in each field in the form.

To access the data, click on the first letter of the name entered in the Last Name field. For example, click on "S" to turn to the names that begin with S. Then, if necessary, turn the page until the entry you want is displayed.

Saving Your Data

All the data you enter in Organizer's datebook is placed in the same file when you save the datebook to a file name. However, you can create as many Organizer files as you wish.

NOTE

Click on the New button on the displayed SmartIcons to open a new, blank Organizer file if you want to create another file for your data. For example, you can create separate files for your business and personal contacts.

1. Click on the Save button on the displayed SmartIcons to display the File Save As dialog box, shown in Figure 23.5.

2. Type a name for the file in the File text box. For example, type **EVRGREEN**. Organizer automatically adds the .ORG file extension.

3. Click on OK to save the file.

OK

FIGURE 23.5

Display the File Save As dialog box to specify a name for your Organizer file.

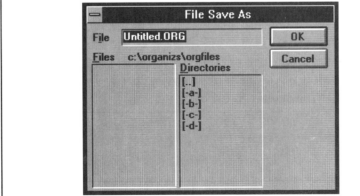

Each time you make an entry in the datebook, be sure you click on the Save button on the displayed SmartIcons to save the file to the same file name.

To automatically open the file each time you start Organizer, click on the Open button on the displayed SmartIcons, click on the name of the file in the Files list box, select the Open Automatically check box, and then click on OK.

Exiting or Minimizing Organizer

After you have saved any changes you made to an Organizer file, you can exit Organizer. However, if you set an alarm for an appointment, minimize Organizer instead so the alarm will sound at the appropriate time.

- To exit Organizer, click on the Exit button on the displayed SmartIcons.

- To minimize Organizer, click on the Minimize button on the right side of the title bar. Organizer is reduced to an icon at the bottom of your screen.

7

Working Together

CHAPTER TWENTY-FOUR

Working Together

ONE OF THE best reasons to use Lotus SmartSuite is that all the applications are integrated—you can enter data in one of the SmartSuite applications and use it in another. For example, you can import data entered into a 1-2-3 worksheet into an Approach database, or you can import data from Approach into a 1-2-3 worksheet.

SmartSuite comes with the Working Together Bonus Pack, a SmartIcon set found in Ami Pro. The Bonus Pack SmartIcons allow you to easily copy data you entered in 1-2-3, Freelance Graphics, and Organizer to or from Ami Pro. Use buttons on the SmartCenter SmartIcon set to start or to switch to any of the SmartSuite applications.

Using the
Working Together Bonus Pack

Follow these steps to get started using the SmartSuite applications together:

1. Click on the Start Lotus Ami Pro button on the SmartCenter SmartIcon set to start Ami Pro.

2. Click on the SmartIcons button on the status bar, and then select Bonus Pack to display the Bonus Pack SmartIcon set.

To display all of the Bonus Pack SmartIcons, select Tools ➤ SmartIcons, click on the Position drop-down button, select Floating in the list box, and then click on OK. Floating Smart-Icons can be dragged to any location in the Ami Pro window.

Using Ami Pro Together with 1-2-3

You can quickly select ranges of data in 1-2-3 and copy them to a new Ami Pro document with the Bonus Pack's Collect & Copy For 1-2-3 button. Collect & Copy For 1-2-3 will start 1-2-3 if it is not running, or activate the 1-2-3 window if it is running.

1. Click on the Collect & Copy For 1-2-3 button on the Bonus Pack SmartIcon set in Ami Pro. The 1-2-3 window appears, along with the Collect & Copy dialog box, shown in Figure 24.1.

2. If necessary, open the file that contains the data you want to copy. For example, open the SALES.WK4 worksheet.

3. Select A4..E7, and then click on Copy To Ami Pro in the Collect & Copy dialog box.

4. Now click on the tab for worksheet B in the SALES.WK4 file and click near the edge of the chart to select it.

5. Click on Copy To Ami Pro again.

6. Click on Done. The Collect & Copy dialog box changes, as shown in Figure 24.2.

FIGURE 24.1

The Collect & Copy dialog box appears when you click on the Collect & Copy For 1-2-3 button on the Bonus Pack SmartIcon set.

Collect & Copy

1. Select the range or chart you want to print.
2. Choose Copy to Ami Pro.
3. Repeat these steps if you want.

Copy to Ami Pro

Done

The Collect & Copy dialog box changes when you are finished copying the selected ranges.

7. Click on Switch To Ami Pro to return to the Ami Pro document. The data and chart you copied appear in the document window, which is reduced to Full Page view on your screen.

Both the data and the chart were copied as *embedded objects* to a new Ami Pro document. An embedded object is created in a *source* (in this case 1-2-3) and placed in a *client* (Ami Pro). Embedded objects can be edited from within the client application.

Objects in Ami Pro are automatically placed in frames. To edit the data or the chart in Ami Pro, double-click on the frame that contains the object to start (or activate) 1-2-3 and open the file that contains the data and chart. Make the necessary changes, and then save them to the 1-2-3 file. The changes will automatically appear in the embedded object in the Ami Pro document.

Creating a Freelance Screen Show from Ami Pro

You can have Freelance Graphics automatically create a screen show with text that is selected in an Ami Pro document.

N O T E

You can also collect pages in a running Freelance presentation and copy them to an Ami Pro document. Click on the Collect & Copy For Freelance button on the Bonus Pack SmartIcon set to select one or more pages of a presentation in Page Sorter view and copy them to the same page in an Ami Pro document.

---

1. Select File ➤ Open (Ctrl+O) to display the Open dialog box, select MERCURY.SAM in the Files list box, and click on OK.

2. Select all the text on the first page starting with the "Ami Pro: The Choice for Mercury Sports" paragraph title.

3. Click on the Screen Show button on the Bonus Pack SmartIcon set. Freelance Graphics automatically starts if it is not running.

4. Select the SmartMaster set for the background of the screen show in the Choose A Look For Your Presentation dialog box. For example, select SPOTLITE.MAS, and then click on OK. The first screen of the show automatically appears.

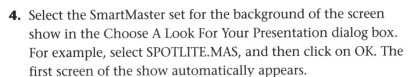

5. Press ↵ to display the next page. Repeat this step for each page until the Freelance Graphics Outliner view is displayed on your screen with the Ami Pro Screen Show dialog box, shown in Figure 24.3.

6. Click on Yes to return to the Ami Pro document.

FIGURE 24.3

When the screen show is finished, the Ami Pro Screen Show dialog box appears, asking if you are ready to return to Ami Pro.

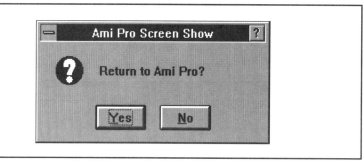

N O T E

You can also create a Freelance organizational chart from within Ami Pro. Position the insertion point in your document where you want the organizational chart to appear, and then click on the Organizational Chart button on the Bonus Pack SmartIcon set. Choose a style for the chart and click on OK. Then type the entries and click on OK to place the chart in your document.

Creating an Organizer Calendar in Ami Pro

The data and appointments you enter in the Calendar in an Organizer file can be used to automatically create a printed version of the calendar in Ami Pro.

1. Click on the Start Lotus Organizer button on the SmartCenter SmartIcon set to start Organizer.

2. If necessary, open the file that contains the calendar you want to print.

3. Press Alt+Tab to switch back to Ami Pro.

4. Click on the Organizer Calendar button on the Bonus Pack SmartIcon set. The Monthly Organizer Calendar dialog box, shown in Figure 24.4, appears.

5. If necessary, click on the Month drop-down button to display a list, and then select the month for which you want the calendar.

6. If necessary, click on the Year drop-down list and select the year of the calendar you want to create.

7. Click on OK to have Ami Pro automatically create the calendar.

FIGURE 24.4

The Monthly Organizer Calendar dialog box appears when the ORGCAL.SMM macro is played.

Monthly Organizer Calendar

This feature creates a monthly calendar using appointment entries in Lotus Organizer.

1. Load the Organizer.
2. Open the Organizer file for which you want to create a calendar.
3. Choose this 'Monthly Organizer Calendar' feature and choose a month and a year for the calendar.

Month : August

Year : 1994

☒ Include Anniversary entries

OK

Cancel

OK

The Organizer Calendar macro takes a little while to run, depending on how much data is in the calendar for the specified month. While it is running, several dialog boxes appear. Do not do anything until the final dialog box appears, telling you that the calendar is ready. Then click on OK to remove the dialog box and select View ➤ Custom to enlarge the calendar (so you can read it) on your screen.

To edit the calendar, click in either the date or the entry text box to position the insertion point, and then use the regular editing methods to insert, replace, or delete text. You can also save the calendar to a file and print it, just as you would any other Ami Pro document.

Go Ahead and Experiment

Now that you have the general idea of how the Lotus SmartSuite Working Together Bonus Pack works, you can try out some of the other Smart-Icons on the Bonus Pack Smarticon set. The set contains SmartIcons you can use to calculate various formulas using 1-2-3's @functions, copy Ami Pro styles to a 1-2-3 worksheet, and even create curved (or otherwise enhanced) text objects. Don't be afraid to experiment with the Bonus Pack. After all, you don't have to save any of your creations!

ndex

Note to the Reader: **Boldfaced** page numbers indicate primary discussions of a topic. *Italicized* page numbers indicate illustrations.

E

GET A FREE CATALOG JUST FOR EXPRESSING YOUR OPINION.

Help us improve our books and get a *FREE* full-color catalog in the bargain. Please complete this form, pull out this page and send it in today. The address is on the reverse side.

Name _____   **Company** _____

Address _____   **City** _____ **State** ____ **Zip** _____

Phone (___) _____

1. **How would you rate the overall quality of this book?**

- ❑ Excellent
- ❑ Very Good
- ❑ Good
- ❑ Fair
- ❑ Below Average
- ❑ Poor

2. **What were the things you liked most about the book? (Check all that apply)**

- ❑ Pace
- ❑ Format
- ❑ Writing Style
- ❑ Examples
- ❑ Table of Contents
- ❑ Index
- ❑ Price
- ❑ Illustrations
- ❑ Type Style
- ❑ Cover
- ❑ Depth of Coverage
- ❑ Fast Track Notes

3. **What were the things you liked *least* about the book? (Check all that apply)**

- ❑ Pace
- ❑ Format
- ❑ Writing Style
- ❑ Examples
- ❑ Table of Contents
- ❑ Index
- ❑ Price
- ❑ Illustrations
- ❑ Type Style
- ❑ Cover
- ❑ Depth of Coverage
- ❑ Fast Track Notes

4. **Where did you buy this book?**

- ❑ Bookstore chain
- ❑ Small independent bookstore
- ❑ Computer store
- ❑ Wholesale club
- ❑ College bookstore
- ❑ Technical bookstore
- ❑ Other _____

5. **How did you decide to buy this particular book?**

- ❑ Recommended by friend
- ❑ Recommended by store personnel
- ❑ Author's reputation
- ❑ Sybex's reputation
- ❑ Read book review in _____
- ❑ Other _____

6. **How did you pay for this book?**

- ❑ Used own funds
- ❑ Reimbursed by company
- ❑ Received book as a gift

7. **What is your level of experience with the subject covered in this book?**

- ❑ Beginner
- ❑ Intermediate
- ❑ Advanced

8. **How long have you been using a computer?**

years _____

months _____

9. **Where do you most often use your computer?**

- ❑ Home
- ❑ Work

- ❑ Both
- ❑ Other _____

10. **What kind of computer equipment do you have? (Check all that apply)**

- ❑ PC Compatible Desktop Computer
- ❑ PC Compatible Laptop Computer
- ❑ Apple/Mac Computer
- ❑ Apple/Mac Laptop Computer
- ❑ CD ROM
- ❑ Fax Modem
- ❑ Data Modem
- ❑ Scanner
- ❑ Sound Card
- ❑ Other _____

11. **What other kinds of software packages do you ordinarily use?**

- ❑ Accounting
- ❑ Databases
- ❑ Networks
- ❑ Apple/Mac
- ❑ Desktop Publishing
- ❑ Spreadsheets
- ❑ CAD
- ❑ Games
- ❑ Word Processing
- ❑ Communications
- ❑ Money Management
- ❑ Other _____

12. **What operating systems do you ordinarily use?**

- ❑ DOS
- ❑ OS/2
- ❑ Windows
- ❑ Apple/Mac
- ❑ Windows NT
- ❑ Other _____

13. On what computer-related subject(s) would you like to see more books?

_____

_____

_____

_____

14. Do you have any other comments about this book? (Please feel free to use a separate piece of paper if you need more room)

_____

_____

_____

_____

PLEASE FOLD, SEAL, AND MAIL TO SYBEX

SYBEX INC.
Department M
2021 Challenger Drive
Alameda, CA
94501

**Your Pushbutton Roadmap to Lotus SmartSuite
in a full-color,
pull-out poster!**

the Pushbutton Guide to

LOTUS SmartSuite

SmartIcon
category

STANDARD SMARTICONS

Paste
Paste ▶ Edit
Ctrl + V

Pastes the Clipboard contents
at the insertion point

Button name

Menu
comman·

Paste

Paste ▶ Edit
Ctrl + V ◀

Pastes the Clipboard contents
at the insertion point

Keybo·
shorto·

Description of the
button's function